Convertibles

Dennis Adler

CRESTLINE

This edition published in 2015 by
CRESTLINE
an imprint of Book Sales
a division of Quarto Publishing Group USA Inc.
142 West 36th Street, 4th Floor
New York, New York 10018
USA

First published in 2011 by Motorbooks, an imprint of Printed with permission of and by arrangement with Motorbooks, an imprint of Quarto Publishing Group USA Inc. 400 First Avenue North, Suite 400, Minneapolis, MN 55401 USA

Library of Congress Cataloging-in-Publication Data

Adler, Dennis, 1948–
Convertibles / Dennis Adler.
    p. cm.
ISBN 978-0-7858-3344-4
1. Automobiles, Convertible—Pictorial works.
2. Automobiles, Convertible—History. I. Title.
TL15.A345 2011
629.222—dc22

2010050553

Editor: Jeffrey Zuehlke
Design Manager: Kou Lor
Series designed by: Laura Rades
Layout by: Mandy Kimlinger

Printed in China

On the frontispiece: 1947 Bentley MX VI Franay Cabriolet.

On the title page: 2011 Ford Mustang GT Convertible. *Ford Motor Company*

CONTENTS

INTRODUCTION

Sounds can evoke vivid mental images of objects, or of the people who create them. The haunting rhythm of a Fender Stratocaster played by Eric Clapton—unmistakable. So too the primitive rumble of a Harley-Davidson trying to catch its breath, the thwack of a Louisville Slugger thundering into the leather hide of a baseball, or the siren song of a convertible racing down the wind with its engine at full cry and the rush of the air pouring over the windshield. Most of us will never play a Fender Stratocaster or hit one out of the park with a Louisville Slugger, but look around every summer, or when the weather is favorable, and you'll see Harleys and convertibles on the road by the thousands. Ironically, motorcycles and convertibles have a great deal in common; both began in the primitive days of motorized transportation, and, like motorcycles, the first motorcars left drivers exposed to the elements.

Many Americans think that Henry Ford invented the automobile at the turn of the last century. Of course, he didn't. It's hard to say if anyone really *invented* the motorcar at all. Ford did make it better and more accessible to more people; and all his early motorcars were touring or open cars, automobiles with fabric tops held by hinged wooden or metal frameworks dating back to the horse-and-buggy era. At best, these were still fair-weather automobiles.

If you go back to the known origins of the horseless carriage you find German engine builder Carl Benz, who took the ideas of several mechanics, bicycle makers, and his own design for a lightweight, single-cylinder engine and, in 1885, behind the doors of his small workshop in Mannheim, built what has since come to be regarded as the first motorized carriage. In January 1886 he received a patent for his *motorwagen* and earned the rather dubious distinction of being the *inventor* of the automobile. Had he waited just a little longer, Benz would have had to share the honor with Gottlieb Daimler and Karl Maybach, two engine builders working 100 kilometers away in the distant town of Cannstatt—less than an hour's drive today. In the twenty-first century, the names Benz, Daimler, and Maybach are the three most closely associated with the invention we call the automobile, but there were so many more.

Personally, I like to think of Henry Ford as the inventor of something much more exciting than the automobile. Yes, he created what history regards as the first moving assembly line (although there is debate even on that point), and he most certainly put America on wheels in 1908 with the Model T, but he built something else, back in 1901, two years before the Ford Motor Company even existed, something that few people at the time recognized as a turning point in the evolution of the automobile. Henry Ford built a sports car.

He wasn't alone. In the same year Ford assembled a racer named *Sweepstakes*, Daimler introduced the first automobile to bear the Mercedes name—a swift, 40-horsepower sports two-seater that swept the racing and hill-climb events at Nice Week in March and wrote itself into history as the first modern automobile. Both were what we would regard today as roadsters. The proper terminology back in the day would have been "runabout." Neither the Ford nor the Mercedes pretended to be anything but racing cars in 1901, but their designs led to the first practical motorcars, nearly all of which were accompanied by some form of folding fabric top to offer the driver and passengers some—albeit very little—protection from the elements.

In 1902 Ford built another speed machine, this one driven to a new threshold of performance by a daredevil named Barney Oldfield. Suddenly, everyone was aware that these noisy, foul-smelling mechanical carriages emerging from every corner of the country might indeed amount to something. These pioneering racers and their sporting cars created something very tangible: curiosity.

By the early 1900s, the automobile had progressed from a novelty into a means of practical personal transportation—at least for those with the means to afford a motorcar. Henry Ford would change that too, with the introduction of the Model T, an affordable two-door runabout offered in any color, so long as it was black. The price in 1909 was a reasonable $825. By 1915 it was down to $440. The everyman's car was a convertible.

As America entered the second decade of the twentieth century, the nation's infrastructure was undergoing revolutionary changes. Horse-drawn carriages still outnumbered motorcars, but the Main Streets of America were seeing more and more autos sharing the thoroughfare each year. And as passenger cars grew in popularity, so too did the charisma of the open-bodied, two-seat sports car.

Throughout turn-of-the-century Europe, sports car racing had gone beyond America's early flirtations with speed, owing to the greater number of paved roads and the long-standing rivalries among nations to prove their superiority over one another. Motor racing was vastly more practical than war, and generally more entertaining. As might be expected, the lines were primarily drawn between France, England, Germany, and Italy, all

1923 Hispano-Suiza H6B Cabriolet.

Austin-Healey 100-6.

of which had enterprising automakers and national pride—the fundamental motivation for building and racing sports cars.

On the other side of the Atlantic, the first 500-mile (805-kilometer) race was held at the new speedway in Indianapolis, Indiana, in 1911. On board tracks across the length and breadth of the land, men were pitting their skills against each other, and sportsmen were taking to the open road with the latest, fastest, and best-designed open two-seaters of the day.

Throughout the early years of the 20th century, the sports car was in the simplest form it would ever be—minimal bodywork, two seats, and the wind in your face. Whether you were driving at Indy or down a country road in upstate New York, in the early 1900s, the line that divided runabouts from race cars was all but nonexistent.

In Mercer County, New Jersey, the Mercer Motorcar Company set the American road on fire in 1911 with a model called the Raceabout. Stutz, in Indianapolis, Indiana, followed suit with a racy model named the Bearcat, and soon every young buck with a toolbox and a few spare dollars was trying to build a sporty two-seater.

Like the motorcar itself, the sports car was in constant change. By the early 1900s, one could simply purchase a speedster body and mount it on a Model T chassis, rebuild the flathead Ford motor, and handcraft a sports car at home (after World War II, this car would evolve into another

American phenomenon—the hot rod), but most men, and a handful of adventuresome women, chose to purchase one of the established sporting cars of the day, such as the Mercer, Stutz, or Marmon. Those of extraordinary wealth either imported the best sporting models from Europe or acquired bare chassis and had them mounted with hand-built roadster and racing bodies of exceptional quality, leading to one of the most exciting eras in all of automotive history.

Within the narrow limits that defined a sports car—or perhaps what was better characterized during the 1930s as a "sporting car"—were the models of European automakers such as Mercedes-Benz (created by the merger of independent automakers Daimler and Benz in 1926), Alfa Romeo, Jaguar, Hispano-Suiza, Isotta Fraschini, Voisin, Bugatti, Delage, Delahaye, and Talbot-Lago. In the United States, a handful of sports models were produced by the nation's foremost automakers, including Cadillac and Lincoln—and by an independent manufacturer in Indianapolis that would leave the most indelible mark on the 1930s of any American automaker: Duesenberg.

By the time of the Great Depression, the sports car had evolved into a singular idea, that of a two-seat (with the occasional rumble seat) model with sleek, open coachwork, a fabric top (and occasionally side curtains), and the most powerful engine its maker could shoehorn beneath the hood. It was not uncommon to find V-12, V-16, and supercharged straight eights powering lightweight roadsters and speedsters. Unfortunately, what were less common in the 1930s were buyers for such cars. Some of the greatest automobiles in history arrived at the worst possible time, during the Great Depression.

By the early 1930s, the sports car had taken a turn down a different road from purebred racing cars. One could race a sports car, but race

cars (Grand Prix cars) were now built solely for competition, making them mostly unsuitable for the open road. It was a brief but exciting era that came to a hasty end in September 1939 when World War II began in Europe, but the desire to build swift, agile-handling cars could not be deterred by war, and less than a year after the hostilities had ceased in Europe (and the Pacific), automakers were dusting off the ruins of their industry, righting drafting tables, rebuilding metal and wood shops, and setting about creating a new postwar generation of automobiles. And many of them would be convertibles.

In the post–World War II era, the sports car as we know it today began to appear as a smaller, more purpose-built design, with the form and function that European automakers had begun to establish in the late 1930s with cars like the MG TB, Alfa Romeo's sporty 6C 2500, and Mercedes-Benz sport roadsters.

In England, the Jaguar XK-120 emerged in 1948 as one of the first modern sports cars of the postwar era. From a small converted sawmill in Austria, the first 356 Porsche saw the light of day, and an Italian emigrant named Luigi Chinetti, who had become a U.S. citizen during the war, returned briefly to Italy to help an old friend, Enzo Ferrari, establish a company that would build sports cars of unparalleled performance and beauty.

Between the dawn of the twentieth century and the end of World War II, the automobile became a necessity for transportation, commerce, and most assuredly pleasure. If nothing else, one thing had become perfectly clear in the minds of manufacturers, designers, and consumers on both sides of the Atlantic: if the automobile satisfied our needs, then a convertible fulfilled our passions. The sight of one on the open road, or even just sitting on a dealer's showroom floor, could make your pulse quicken and your breath catch—and make you whisper to yourself, "I want one."

CHAPTER 1
IN THE BEGINNING— DAWN OF THE TWENTIETH CENTURY

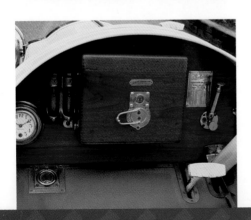

In the beginning there was light—literally. Motorcars didn't have tops. This was remedied by the early 1900s with the use of folding fabric (leather or canvas) tops based, not surprisingly, on surrey tops of the late nineteenth century, largely because most of the early coachbuilders manufacturing bodies for automobiles had started out in the carriage trade. Even so, most automakers, both in the United States and abroad, continued to sell motorcars without tops, and did so well into the mid-1910s. Sporting cars simply looked better that way. How often do you see a modern convertible on the road with the top up?

To understand convertibles, you have to go back to the beginning, when every car was, in essence, a convertible, whether or not it actually had a folding fabric top. This is where specific terminologies, mostly European in origin, come from. The use of the word "convertible" is very American. In England convertibles are called "dropheads"; in Italy, a country that knows a thing or two about convertibles, they are called "spyders," or "spiders" in the parlance of Alfa Romeo, though most Italian automakers—even Ferrari—have come around to using the *i* in place of the *y* in recent times.

January 29, 2006, marked the 120th anniversary of the first motorcar, at least as we have come to regard it. In truth it was a motorized tricycle, and if you look on the highway today, you will see them by the thousands, many powered by Harley-Davidson engines; not exactly what Carl Benz might have envisioned in 1885, but the idea is

pretty much the same. Benz believed that a man should not be limited in his ability to travel by the constraints of steel rails or the shortcomings of horse-drawn carriages. To be truly free, he said, one must not be encumbered by schedules and routes or by the stamina of horses. Thus Benz took to task the idea of motorized personal transportation in the mid-1880s.

In 1885 the gasoline engine was not a new idea. Large, stationary engines had been used to power industrial and farm machinery since the latter part of the century, and in fact Carl Benz had pioneered their development. It was his conception of a small, single-cylinder version, however, that allowed him to create a phenomenon—the motorized carriage we know today as the 1886 Benz Patent Motorwagen (right).

By the turn of the last century, motorcars had graduated to four wheels, and in Europe, where the motor carriage had been born, open cars were often called touring models. Thus our tale of the convertible begins in Europe in 1901, when Daimler Motoren Gesellschaft introduced the first Mercedes.

The transition from the horseless carriage pioneered in 1885 by Carl Benz to the automobile came hurriedly. What began in 1897 with the cumbersome, front-engine Daimler Phoenix (the first production motorcar to put the engine up front) evolved into the first modern motorcar, the Mercedes, in March 1901. The new Daimler model, named after investor Emil Jellinek's young daughter, was unveiled at the annual Speed Trials and La Turbie hill climb along France's luxurious Côte d'Azure. Built on a longer, lower chassis and fitted with trend-setting coachwork, the 1901 Mercedes weighed only 2,200 pounds (1,000

1901 MERCEDES

Price: N/A
Engine: Four-cylinder T-head
Displacement: 5.9 liters (360 cubic inches)
Output: 35 horsepower
Gearbox: Four-speed gated gear transmission
Production: 36

kilograms), almost half the weight of the Phoenix, and was powered by a new 5.9-liter (360-cubic-inch), T-head, four-cylinder engine producing

35 horsepower. Daimler factory driver Wilhelm Werner drove the Mercedes up La Turbie hill on March 29 at an unprecedented speed of 31.9 miles per hour (51.3 kilometers per hour) and drove flat out in the distance race at a blistering 55 miles per hour (88.5 km/hr), leaving every other contender far behind. The Mercedes was already a legend before the end of the annual competition in Nice and was hailed in the motor press as a sensation.

The production models of the 1901 Mercedes introduced a steel chassis, a honeycomb radiator in front of the engine, a gated four-speed gear-change lever, driven rear wheels, and two- or four-passenger seating, a simple formula that has prevailed, with few changes to the basic concept, for over a century. By 1903, when Mercedes won its third Le Turbie title, almost every other motorcar in the world was obsolete in terms of design, and automakers on both sides of the Atlantic had begun rethinking the very idea of an automobile.

Did You Know?

The 1901 Mercedes was the first mass-produced motorcar to have a honeycomb radiator and the first automobile with a four-speed, gated gear change. When the Mercedes was introduced, Emil Jellinek, Daimler's sales agent in France, agreed to purchase the first 36 cars built at a cost of 550,000 gold marks, around $130,000 in 1900. He sold every one of them!

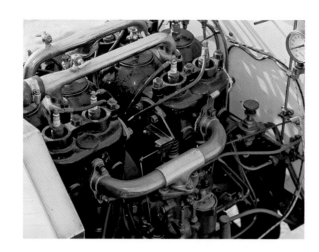

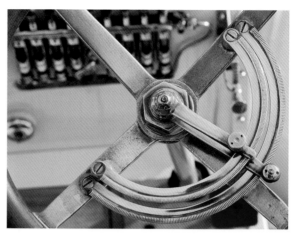

Packard, Peerless, and Pierce-Arrow were three of America's earliest prestige motorcars. All three sold for an average price of $5,000, which was roughly the cost of a very nice home in the early twentieth century.

Peerless introduced its first motorcar at Madison Square Garden in 1902, setting its sights on America's wealthiest. The manufacturer's advertising boldly stated that Peerless was "the car that goes when you want it to go—where you want to go—as fast as you want to go, and stops only when you want it to stop. It runs smoothly, noiselessly, without perceptible vibration—is simple in mechanical construction—easily controlled and luxurious

1903 PEERLESS TYPE 6 REAR ENTRANCE TONNEAU

Price: N/A

Engine: Two-cylinder vertical twin

Displacement: 194.9 cubic inches (3.19 liters)

Output: 16 horsepower

Gearbox: Sliding gear transmission

Production: 547

in its appointments." What else could a car owner ask for? The 1903 Type 6 Rear Entrance Tonneau pictured here is a flawlessly restored example from the Nethercutt Collection.

Did You Know?

This beautifully restored 1903 Peerless was driven in the 1984 London-to-Brighton Run by its former owner, 1961 Formula 1 World Champion Phil Hill. The vertical twin engine delivers 16 horsepower and uses shaft drive to the rear axle, an uncommon feature in 1903.

1903 PEERLESS TYPE 6 REAR ENTRANCE TONNEAU

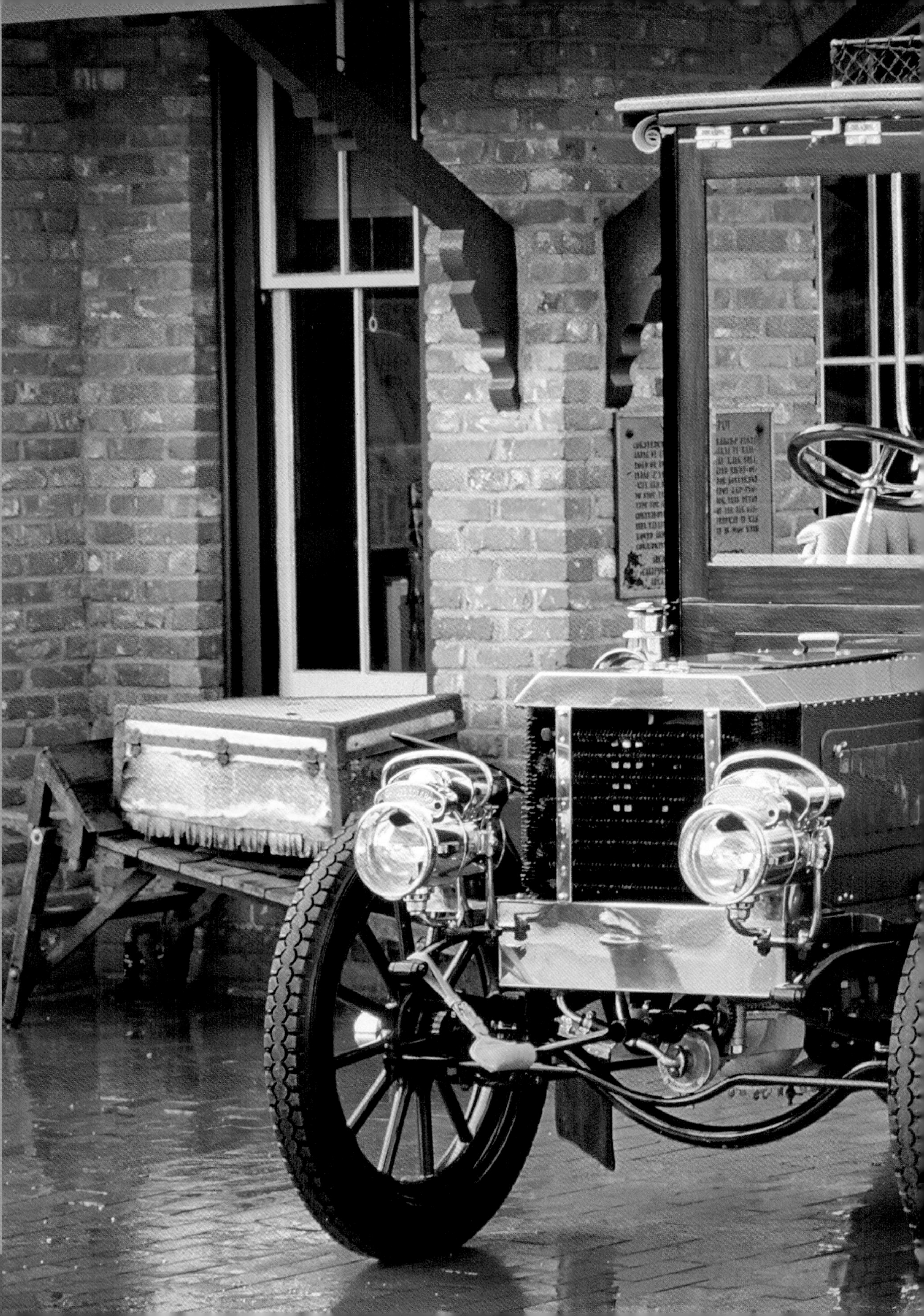

"Please move to the front of the vehicle." The rear entrance design was all the rage in the early 1900s, and this handsome 1904 Packard Model L Rear Entrance Tonneau on display in the Nethercutt Collection in Sylmar, California, was one of the most elegant of early American motorcars. The tonneau was powered by a 241.7-cubic-inch (3.96-liter) L-head four-cylinder engine, with an output of 22 horsepower. Its body, hood, and fenders were all hand-formed aluminum.

1904 PACKARD MODEL L REAR ENTRANCE TONNEAU

Price: $3,000
Engine: L-head four-cylinder
Displacement: 241.7 cubic inches (3.96 liters)
Output: 22 horsepower
Gearbox: Sliding gear transmission
Production: N/A

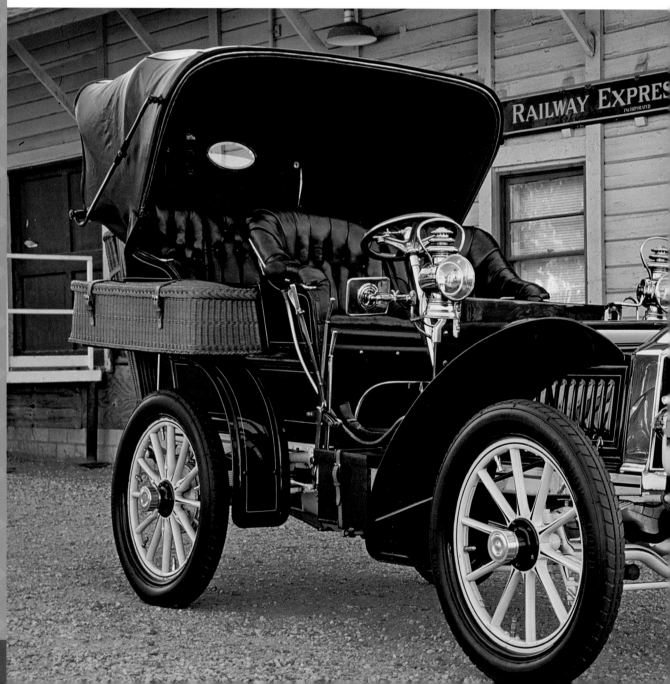

Beginning at 6:16 p.m. on August 6, 1904, driver Charles Schmidt ran a Model L Packard around the Grosse Point, Michigan, track for 29 hours, 53 minutes, 37.6 seconds, averaging 33.5 miles per hour (54 km/hr), to set a record as the first car to travel 1,000 miles (1,609 km) without shutting off the engine. The only stops were for tires and fuel, during which the engine was left running. At the time it was an unparalleled achievement.

Did You Know?

Packard was an innovator in automobile design and engineering. The 1904 Model L was constructed with an all-aluminum body, hood, and fenders. The headlamps are Model 45 Gray & Davis "bullets," and the side lamps are Solar 41a's. Since the electric headlight had not yet been invented, automobile lights were powered by acetylene gas, produced by combining water and calcium carbide in a separate tank mounted on the running board. A match was required to light the headlights and running lights for an evening drive!

Early motorists had to make some interesting decisions when purchasing an automobile, including choosing between three very different means of propulsion: electric, steam, or gasoline. While the internal combustion engine was being developed in the late 1890s, American and European automakers were also experimenting with electric and steam engines as alternative power sources. Electrics, however, were strictly city cars with limited range and equally limited appeal. For the majority of motorists it really came down to a choice between gas and steam, and for a brief time in the automobile's history steam was a very

1906 STANLEY STEAMER MODEL F TOURING

Price: N/A
Engine: Steam powered twin-piston, double-acting type
Displacement: 184 cubic inches (3 liters)
Output: 20 horsepower
Gearbox: Hand-operated accelerator
Production: N/A

viable alternative. They made sense to most people because steam engines had powered locomotives in America since 1825. It was the Stanley brothers,

Francis and Freelan, of Newton, Massachusetts, who put steam power to work in a practical automotive design in 1897.

Within ten years, Stanley Steamers like this Model F Touring (one of six different models offered in 1906) numbered in the thousands and steam had become the greatest competitor to the internal combustion engine. As road cars, the Stanley Steamers gave up little to conventional automobiles, other than a longer and more difficult starting process, which required heating the boiler for about 20 minutes before getting underway. Every bit the equal of gasoline-powered automobiles, and fitted with lightweight coachwork, sporting models such as the Gentleman's Speedy Roadster were advertised as the "Fastest Stock Car in the World." The roadster was capable of reaching the then much touted "mile a minute" with its two-cylinder, 20-horsepower steam engine. *Car from the John McMullen Collection*

Did You Know?

In 1906 a streamlined Stanley driven by the great Fred Marriott reached a record speed of 127 miles per hour (204 km/hr) in the Dewar Cup at Ormond Beach, Florida. The following year Marriott crashed the car in a speed trial doing well over 150 miles per hour (241 km/hr)! The driver made a full recovery and lived to the age of 83.

In Germany, Daimler (Mercedes) was leading the European market with the most innovative motorcars of the early twentieth century. The 1900s marked the beginning of an era when enterprise and progress in the development of personal transportation advanced by leaps and bounds. By 1907 models such as the immense Mercedes-Simplex Touring were among the most elegant motorcars in the world. One of the largest models, with seating for up to six, was equipped with individual front seats that offered the style and comfort of easy chairs. Leather upholstery and deep horsehair padding made the driving experience more comfortable, which cannot be said for the stiff suspensions of the era.

Driving was a serious endeavor because there was much to do from behind the wheel besides steering. The instrument board and steering wheel reveal numerous controls that had to be set correctly for both starting and running. On the firewall panel (the dashboard had yet to be invented), next to a white-faced gauge, was a small, round-handled brass pump that required occasional pumping by either the driver or a passenger to keep air pressure in the fuel tank and to maintain the flow of gasoline to the carburetor. Fuel pumps had yet to be invented either.

By this period the Mercedes name had been adopted and was a fixture on the honeycombed radiators. Also note the three-pointed star, already in use on the grille shell of this 1907, two years before DMG received trademark protection for the now famous emblem.

1907 MERCEDES 35 HP TOURING

Price: N/A

Engine: Four-cylinder, water cooled

Displacement: 5.3 liters (319 cubic inches)

Output: 35 horsepower at 950 rpm

Gearbox: Four-speed gated shifter

Production: N/A

Did You Know?

These immense Mercedes Touring cars (Phaeton for six, or Kettenwagen) were built for luxury not speed and featured the most amenities of any car built in Germany, rivaling the British Rolls-Royce Silver Ghosts for fit and finish. This same body style could be ordered with engines producing up to 70 horsepower (Model 38/70 1910–1912) and capable of reaching nearly 60 miles per hour (96 km/hr).

It was referred to as the "Gentlemen's car built by gentlemen." The Packard Model 18 Runabout of 1909 preceded both the Stutz and the Mercer as one of America's earliest sporting motorcars. The Model 18 and the Model 30 (the numbers indicating horsepower) were more elegant in their design than the more race-oriented Mercer or Stutz models that appeared in the 1910s. The Packard's handbrake and three-speed gear change were mounted on the outside of the driver's compartment. The roadsters were built on a Model 18 chassis shortened from 112 to 102 inches (2.84 to 2.59 meters). Another interesting fact is that in the early 1900s, all motorcars, regardless of where they were manufactured,

1909 PACKARD MODEL 18 RUNABOUT

Price: $3,200, plus an additional $25 for the elegant white color scheme
Engine: Four-cylinder T-head
Displacement: 326 cubic inches (5.3 liters)
Output: 18 horsepower
Gearbox: Three-speed sliding gear
Production: Approximately 1,900

whether in the United States by Packard or in Germany by Daimler, were right-hand drive. Left-hand drive didn't appear on American automobiles until around 1915.

Did You Know?

The Model 18 was built on a 112-inch (2.84-m) wheelbase; however, the sporty Runabout was produced on an even shorter 102-inch (2.59-m) platform, riding on 34-inch (86.36-centimeter) tires. A Packard ad in the *Saturday Evening Post* of September 16, 1911, made note that 14 percent of all parties registering at the swank Elton Hotel in Waterbury, Connecticut, were driving Packards—twice as many as any other marque.

36 PACKARD MODEL 18 RUNABOUT

CHAPTER 2
RAGTOPS AND ROADSTERS— 1910 TO 1920

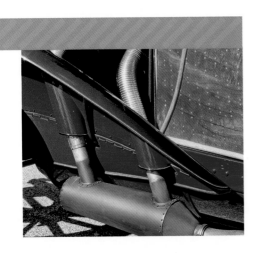

How one defines a convertible depends upon the era in which it was built, and in the 1910s it was built as simply as possible. Early models such as the Mercer Raceabout and Stutz Bearcat were hell on wheels—hairy, thundering machines that were little more than two seats attached to a chassis and engine. The top was an afterthought along with some form of windshield, which in the early 1900s was a round glass "monocle" mounted in front of the driver. It was atop cars such as these that legendary race drivers such as Ralph DePalma, Spencer Wishart, and Barney Oldfield built their reputations.

While convertibles—still a term broadly encompassing any motorcar with a folding top—were often small, sporty two-seaters, or four-place tonneau models, luxurious, full-sized touring cars were the mainstay for most automakers in the 1910s. There were three great names in American luxury motoring: Packard, Peerless, and Pierce-Arrow. Of the three, Pierce-Arrow was often held in the highest esteem among America's upper class. An advertisement for the period read: "The man who looks at a Pierce-Arrow envies the owner for the striking individuality of the car's design. The man who rides in a Pierce-Arrow envies the owner for the car's absolute reliability under all conditions of service. The man who owns a Pierce-Arrow envies no one."

In 1910 Pierce-Arrow, as an automaker, was a year short of a decade old. When founder George N. Pierce retired in 1909, the company, which had built its early reputation manufacturing bicycles, officially became the Pierce-Arrow Motor Car Company. By now Pierce had distinguished itself building cars, which were acclaimed and awarded for their reliable operation. In 1909 Pierce-Arrow won the sought-after Glidden Trophy for the fourth time, as well as the coveted Hower Trophy.

By 1910, when this handsome Model 48 Seven-Passenger Touring was built, the average price of a Pierce-Arrow had reached $5,000, commensurate with competitive models from Packard and Peerless. The Model 48 was powered by Pierce's proven T-head six, which had the cylinders cast in pairs. It was a massive motor displacing 453.2 cubic inches (7.4 l) and developing 48 horsepower. *Car from the Nethercutt Collection*

1910 PIERCE-ARROW MODEL 48 SEVEN-PASSENGER TOURING

Price: $5,000

Engine: Six-cylinder T-head

Displacement: 453.2 cubic inches (7.4 liters)

Output: 48 horsepower

Gearbox: Four-speed sliding gear transmission

Production: Approximately 825

Did You Know?

A Pierce motorcar—a Great Arrow driven by George N. Pierce's son Percy—won the very first Glidden Tour in 1905. The Buffalo, New York, automaker won the Glidden Tour again in 1906 and 1907, failing only in 1908 to make it a complete sweep for five straight years.

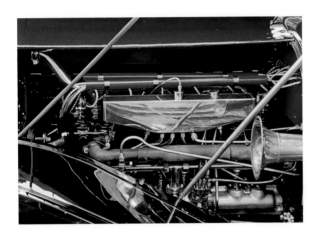

1910 PIERCE-ARROW MODEL 48 SEVEN-PASSENGER TOURING

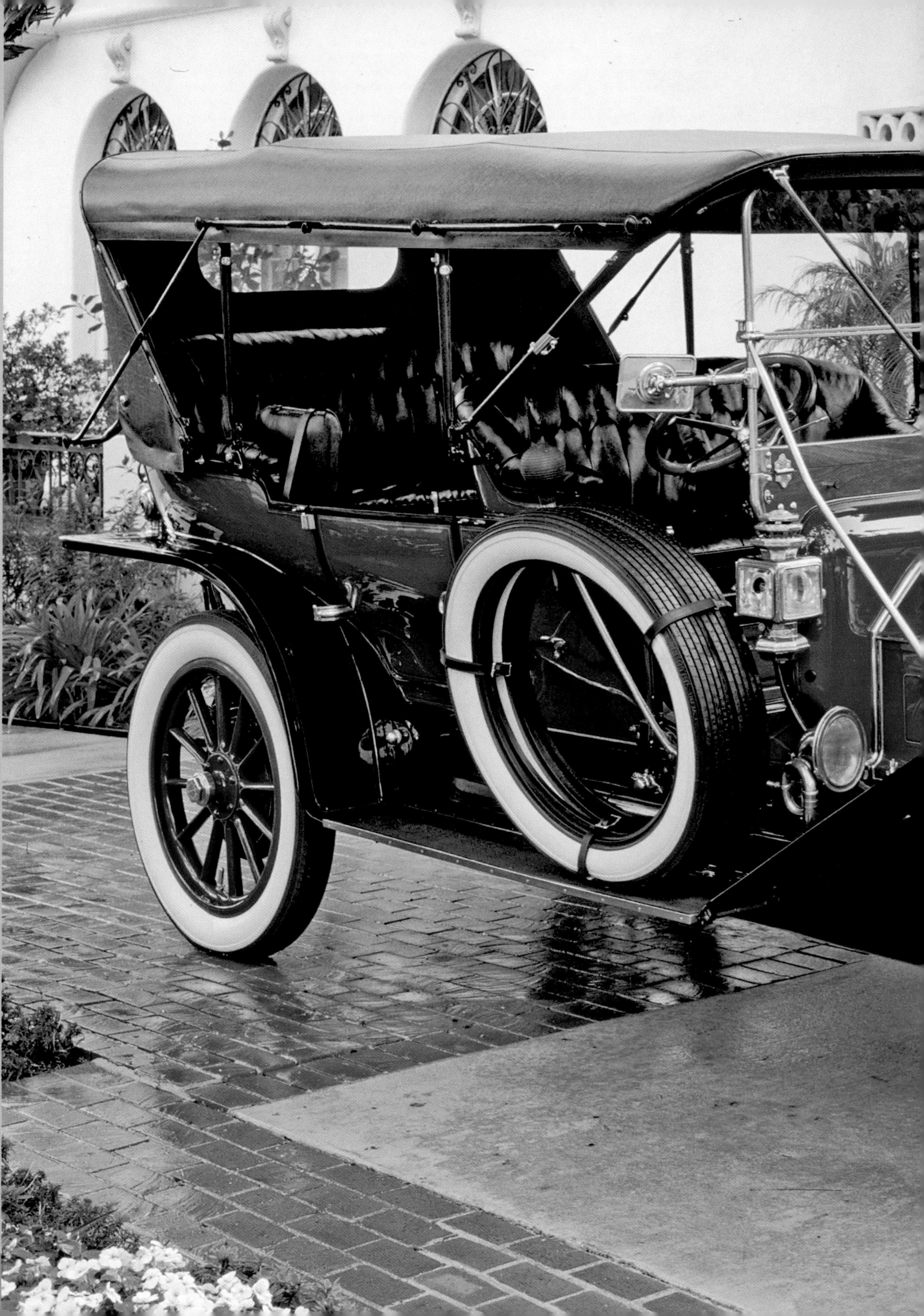

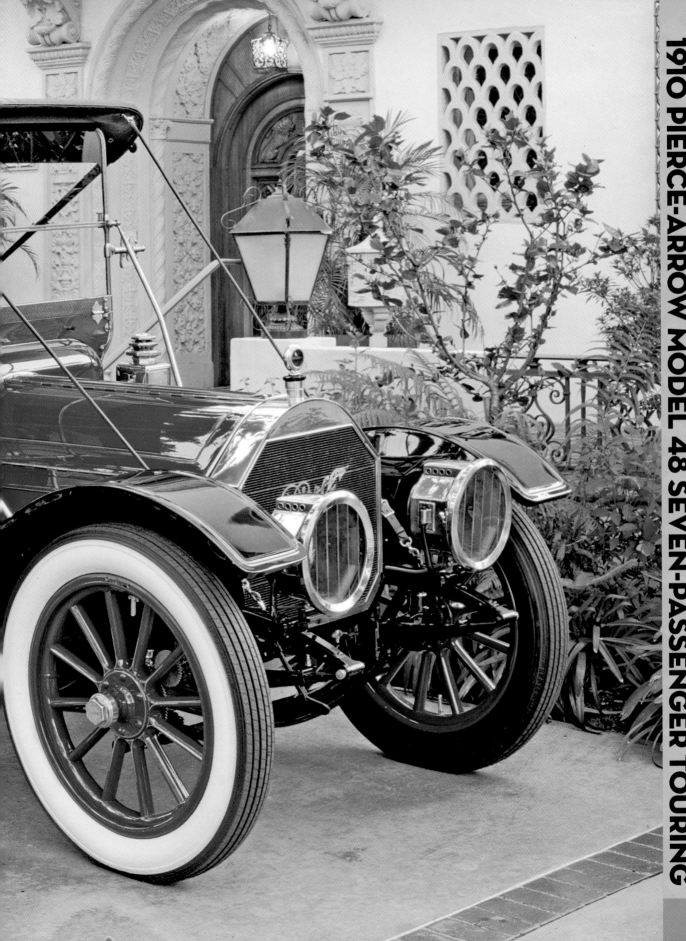

In the early 1910s, Mercedes styling ran the gamut, from conservative formal limousines and landaulets to dashing phaetons and high-spirited sport two-seaters. None, however, approached the styling of the one-off 1911 Model 37/90 Labourdette Skiff, the most exotic nonracing Mercedes built prior to World War I.

In 1910 the Avenue des Champs-Elysées atelier of Henri Labourdette pioneered the exquisite wooden skiff torpedo design—a body style that would become eminently popular in Europe throughout the decade and remain so well into the early 1920s. For Labourdette, wood seemed the most appropriate medium in which to work,

since his skiff design was a boatlike body attached to an automobile chassis. The luster of varnished wood—its color, depth, textures, and grain—appealed to Labourdette in a way mere metal could never match. Certainly, steel was the foundation upon which the automobile was built, and in most cases bodied, but the Labourdette skiff was more. It was a benchmark in the history of early coachbuilding.

The triple-layer body was created by crisscrossing tiers of mahogany over a ribbed frame, then applying a third horizontal layer atop the substructure. To preserve the rigidity, doors were kept as small as possible in number and size. Apart from its attractiveness, a skiff body was light,

normally weighing about 400 pounds (181 kg). The lightness was partly due to the varnished wooden framework being left visible, eliminating the need for interior panels and trim.

Produced from 1910 through 1914, the 37/90 was powered by a four-cylinder engine with two blocks of two cylinders each, with three overhead valves per cylinder and a single camshaft mounted high in the crankcase. Fuel delivery was through a single Mercedes sliding piston carburetor. The average top speed for the cars was estimated at 70 miles per hour (113 km/hr)—although it was reported that with lightweight coachwork, they could reach almost 100 miles per hour (161 km/hr).

1911 MERCEDES 37/90 LABOURDETTE SKIFF

Price: $18,000

Engine: Inline four; three overhead valves per cylinder

Displacement: 9 liters (580 cubic inches)

Output: 90 horsepower

Gearbox: Four-speed, with gate change shifter mounted outside the body

Production: 1

Did You Know?

In the early twentieth century, wood was often used for building automobile bodies, for the framework under body panels, for the bows used to operate the convertible top, for artillery spoke wheels commonly used in the period, and even for the frame on early cars. This 1911 Mercedes, however, was the only wooden-bodied model built.

In 1910 the Mercer Automobile Company was established in Trenton in Mercer County, New Jersey. If Ford was building family cars and Pierce-Arrow luxury touring cars, then Mercer was building sporting cars. The company produced three models: the two-passenger speedster (later named Raceabout), the five-seat touring (with more substantial coachwork), and the toy tonneau four-seater. The Type 35 Raceabout was Mercer's most famous car, and although not endowed with a particularly large engine—just 300 cubic inches (4.9 liters)—or exceptional puissance, the T-head four proved to be quite ample when mounted to the lightweight chassis and rudimentary bodywork. The car was equipped with a superb three-speed selective transmission, improved to a four-speed in 1913, and an oil-wetted multiple-disc clutch, which contributed to the two-seater's agile performance.

Mercer's string of racing victories through 1916 established the company as a leader in early motorsports competition. With Mercer, less was more, and the gossamer bodywork of the Raceabout—advertised as "The Champion Light Car"—was not indicative of its cost, a rather hefty average of $2,500 by 1913.

1911-1913 MERCER RACEABOUT

Price: $2,500

Engine: T-head four

Displacement: 300 cubic inches (4.9 liters)

Output: 30 horsepower

Gearbox: Three-speed selective (1911 and 1912 models); four-speed (1913 model)

Production: Fewer than 1,000

Did You Know?

In 1911 Mercer Raceabouts won five out of six major races in which they were entered. The following year, at the Los Angeles Speedway, Ralph DePalma established eight new world records with a Raceabout, and Spencer Wishart took a Model 35 off the showroom floor of an Ohio dealer and handily won a 200-mile (322-km) race in Columbus, establishing four new dirt-track records in the process. In 1913 a racing model driven by Wishart finished second in the Indianapolis 500.

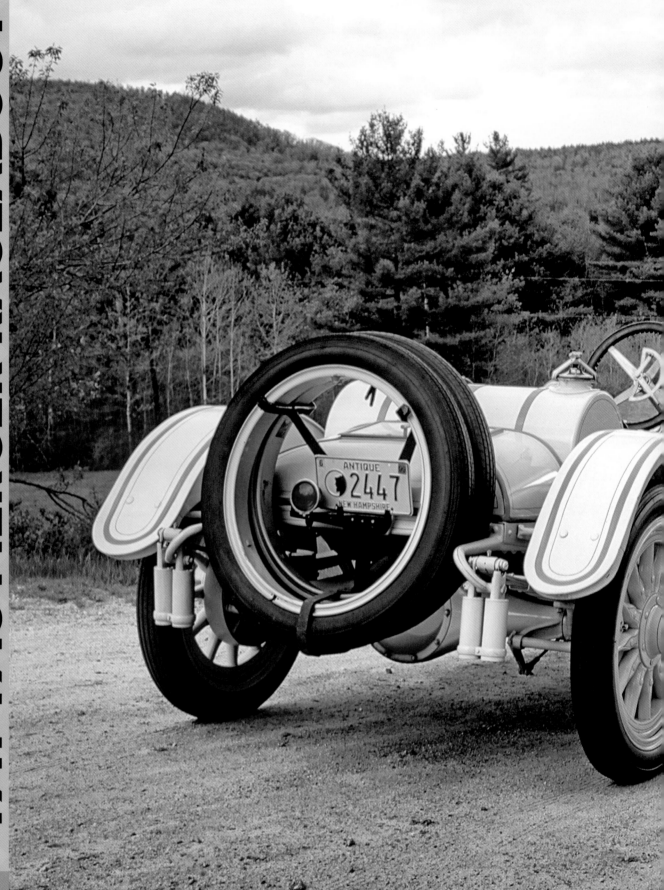

In the early 1910s the first true high-performance motorcars became available to the public. Such machines had previously been built solely for racing, but with the continuing call from consumers for more powerful road cars, automakers such as Daimler began to offer their racing-developed engines for touring cars. The trend had begun with the Model 37/90, but by 1913 models such as this handsomely styled 37/95 (95 horsepower) Double Phaeton, bodied in France by Labourdette, were approaching speeds of 100 miles per hour (161 km/hr). Daimler offered a total of 12 different chassis, 4 with conventional chain-driven rear axles and 8 with the new shaft-drive system.

Shaft drive had been designed by Paul Daimler in 1907, and though chain drive was being phased out, in 1910 the factory introduced a new series of chain-driven cars, including the 37/90 and 37/95 models. Daimler's justification was simply that chain drive had proven more durable in cars equipped with higher-powered engines, such as the 37/95.

The sweeping lines of the Labourdette body, this time made from metal rather than wood, made even the rudimentary enclosed chain-drive mechanisms (forward of the rear fenders) a styling element. The V form Mercedes grille was elegantly set off by a phalanx of corrugated pipes exiting through the

hood and plunging into the exhaust system. The early Mercedes inspired automakers the world over to make exhaust pipes part of an automobile's design.

The car's interior was luxuriously appointed in fine handcrafted woods and leathers, and the driver had at his disposal the most complete series of instruments then available on any motorcar in the world. The dashboard had still not been invented, and all the Mercedes' gauges were spread across an elaborately hand-finished veneer firewall panel. The Mercedes 37/95 was regarded as the most powerful production automobile in the world in 1913.

Car from the Nethercutt Collection

1913 MERCEDES 37/95 DOUBLE PHAETON

Price: N/A

Engine: Inline four

Displacement: 9.5 liters (580 cubic inches)

Output: 95 horsepower

Gearbox: Four-speed with a gate change shifter mounted to the outside of the body

Production: Fewer than 1,000 between 1911 and 1913

Did You Know?

Putting the pedal to the metal in the 1910s took some practice. There were four pedals to deal with: two brake pedals, a clutch pedal, and a small black throttle. Add to this that the shift lever and handbrake were outside the driver's compartment, and you had best have your wits about you!

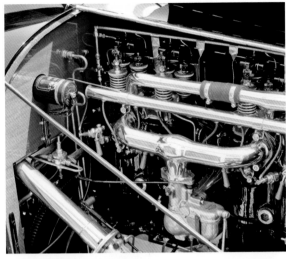

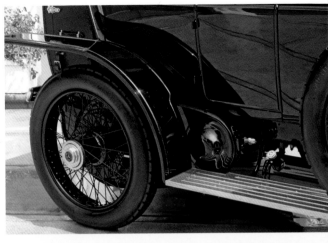

In Great Britain there was only one word for luxury—well, actually two words, Rolls-Royce, created by the amalgamation of C. S. Rolls & Co. and Royce & Co. Ltd., in March 1906. The following year Messrs. Frederick Henry Royce and Charles Stewart Rolls introduced the Silver Ghost, named for the thirteenth car produced, which featured a distinctive gray color scheme and silver-plated fitments. All 40/50 horsepower six-cylinder Rolls-Royce models were known thereafter as Silver Ghosts.

From the onset, Rolls-Royce automobiles set an international standard for quality, luxury, and engineering, and by 1910 the Silver Ghost was the most desirable luxury automobile in the world, a car for monarchs, potentates, and captains of industry. It remained in production until 1924.

1913 ROLLS-ROYCE SILVER GHOST ALPINE TOURER

Price: $6,425 U.S.

Engine: L-head six-cylinder

Displacement: 453.2 cubic inches (7.42 liters)

Output: 40–50 horsepower (estimated)

Gearbox: Four-speed, with a gate change shifter mounted to the outside of the body

Production: 7,874 chassis (manufactured from 1906 to 1926)

The Silver Ghost was an engineering masterpiece, powered by an inline six-cylinder engine with a swept volume of 453.2 cubic inches (7.42 liters) and an output estimated at 50 horsepower. We say "estimated" because Rolls-Royce never published horsepower figures in its sales brochures, stating only that horsepower was adequate.

Elegant and sporty livery such as the 1913 Alpine Tourer commanded a significant price, converted from pounds sterling to about $6,425. Measuring 187 1/4 inches (4.76 m) and tipping the scales at a modest 4,380 pounds/1,987 kilograms (thanks to the lightweight body), the Silver Ghost Alpine Tourer could deliver its passengers to a top speed well in excess of 65 miles per hour (105 km/hr). There were only three original Alpine Tourer bodies built for the Silver Ghost chassis. This 1913 Silver Ghost was originally a limousine and was rebodied into an Alpine Tourer following the original Holms of Derby design. It was not uncommon for a coachbuilt motorcar to have more than one body fitted to its chassis, as the mechanicals often outlasted the coachwork that surrounded them. Some owners preferred to have both a winter (closed) and summer (open) body for the same chassis and to have them switched seasonally! This car was formerly owned by legendary American gun maker William B. Ruger.

Did You Know?

Rolls-Royce did not build bodies for any of its cars until 1939. When a Rolls-Royce Silver Ghost (and later models throughout the 1920s and 1930s) was ordered, it came as a rolling chassis ready for coachwork. The company was always interested in how the various coachbuilders utilized the chassis, and there was a catalog of standardized coachwork from a number of established firms in England and abroad.

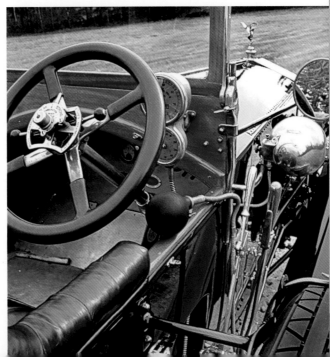

Oakland was incorporated in Pontiac, Michigan, by Edward N. Murphy as the Pontiac Buggy Company in 1891, but it had to be renamed after the rival Pontiac Spring and Wagon Works introduced a motorized high-wheeler under the Pontiac name. Murphy chose Oakland, which he had used for his wagons, and reincorporated in August 1907. Well on the road to success using a 40-horsepower four in his new Oakland models, Murphy was approached by William C. Durant, who had formed General Motors and was buying up companies as fast as he could. Murphy sold out to Durant but never got the chance to enjoy his good fortune. Murphy died shortly after the sale at age 44.

1915 OAKLAND MODEL 37 SPEEDSTER

Price: $1,150

Engine: Four-cylinder

Displacement: 192 cubic inches (3.1 liters)

Output: 40 horsepower

Gearbox: Three-speed selective sliding gear

Production: Approximately 3,500

Once in the GM fold, Oakland quickly began to prosper. The four-cylinder line, consisting of roadster and touring models, became one of GM's

best sellers. By 1913 the Oakland had increased in both size and power, with a 60-horsepower, 334-cubic-inch (5.47-liter) six-cylinder engine under the hood. Nearly 9,000 Oakland models, featuring the new Kettering self-starter and electric lights (more GM advancements), were sold in 1913, and within two years sales were approaching 1,000 cars per month. That figure had doubled by 1916, when an eight-cylinder engine was added.

The 1915 Model 37 Speedster shown here captured the essence of brutish two-seaters like the Mercer Raceabout and Stutz Bearcat but tempered it with extraordinary grace and character, giving up nothing to either competitor. The Oakland Speedster had no trunk, instead using the rear deck to hold dual spares. The car also had no doors—one simply stepped on the running boards, over the short body panels, and into the seat.

Raceabouts like the Oakland Model 37 were not long for the automotive world, as styling, engineering, and performance improvements led to faster and more refined sports cars. Their disappearance marked the end of an era—and with it some of the innocence and rugged adventure that made those first years after the turn of the last century so exciting.

Did You Know?

Oakland remained one of General Motors' best-selling lines and in 1931 became the Pontiac Motor Company division of GM. Although not uncommon for the era, one item absent from the Oakland was an instrument panel fuel gauge. However, GM at least gave drivers something better than a stick to shove down the fuel filler; attached to the fuel tank at the back of the rear deck was a fuel level gauge.

1915
OAKLAND
MODEL 37 SPEEDSTER

It came to be known as the "Dominant Six," but around Packard's East Grand Boulevard factory, everyone called the 1915 Model 5-48 "Jesse Vincent's Hot Rod." The car wasn't intended to be known for its unsurpassed speed, but it turned out that way all the same. In a 1915 Packard advertisement, East Grand's chief engineer Jesse Vincent said, "Be careful how you step on this car. It leaps like a projectile."

With a massive swept volume of 525 cubic inches (8.6 liters) and an output of 80 horsepower, the big six was capable of what Packard called "The Fastest Getaway—60 Miles an Hour in 30 Seconds from a Standing Start." While that may not sound very impressive today, in 1915 it was a startling speed for anything that wasn't built for racing. The last of the series, the 5-48 (also known as the Fifth 48), set a record at the Indianapolis Speedway, clocking 70 miles (113 km) in just one hour. Because of its well-known high-speed capability, the Packard was practically the official getaway car of the

underworld, one that could easily outrun the lower-priced automobiles used by local and state law enforcement agencies.

This elegant 1915 Model 5-48 Seven-Passenger Touring is painted in traditional Packard colors—Richelieu blue and black with yellow trim—and is upholstered in black leather. The 1915 Packard Six radiator cap, a tall stack with an enamel finish and bright red "48" emblem, indicated that this was a six-cylinder model. *Car from the Nethercutt Collection*

1915 PACKARD MODEL 5-48 SEVEN-PASSENGER TOURING

Price: $4,850

Engine: Inline six-cylinder

Displacement: 525 cubic inches (8.6 liters)

Output: 80 horsepower

Gearbox: Three-speed manual

Production: 360

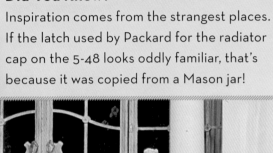

Did You Know?

Inspiration comes from the strangest places. If the latch used by Packard for the radiator cap on the 5-48 looks oddly familiar, that's because it was copied from a Mason jar!

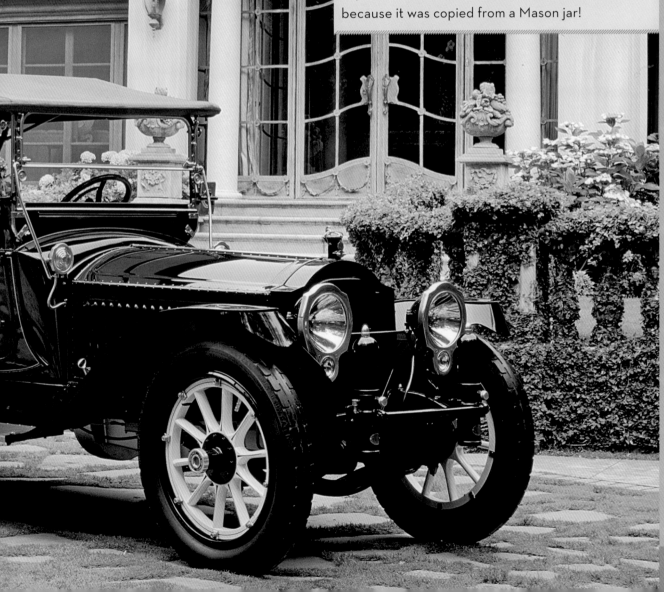

Pierce-Arrow had solidly established itself as one of America's preeminent automakers by 1915, going from strength to strength each year and never shying away from letting its exclusive clientele know about it. A 1915 sales brochure stated, "Discriminating men and women have little patience with compromise. They want the best, always, whether it's food or clothing, a room in a hotel, a cabin on a ship, a horse, or a motorcar. Motorcars are of three kinds: cheap cars, cars of compromise, and cars of quality." It goes without saying where Pierce-Arrow placed itself.

The 1915 model line consisted of no less than 13 different body styles—from the sporty two-passenger Runabout to a regal Vestibule Suburban Landau. All models in the 1915 series 36C, 48B, and 66A, regardless of style or wheelbase, featured the exclusive Pierce-Arrow fender design with integrated headlamps, a Pierce trademark established in 1913 that was literally decades ahead of any other automaker.

This imposing 1915 Model 48B Five-Passenger Touring was one of Pierce-Arrow's most popular body styles, selling for $4,900.

Pierce coachwork for 1915 was highlighted by a trend toward more rounded body lines, larger fenders, and a cowl that flowed from the hood up to the body. To give the cars a more streamlined appearance, the frames were dropped between the axles, and the entire body was lowered by 3 inches (7.62 cm). The famous headlights also received a facelift, the housings redesigned into a concave silhouette that would remain unchanged for the next 18 years.

Under the svelte hood line was an enormous 524.8-cubic-inch (8.6-liter) T-head six that delivered a rousing 48 horsepower. Pierce-Arrow was one of many established American automakers that built automotive bodies in-house, though custom coachwork on the costly, handcrafted motorcars was always an option. The body on this touring model was designed and built in Buffalo by Pierce-Arrow. *Car from the Nethercutt Collection*

1915 PIERCE-ARROW MODEL 48B FIVE-PASSENGER TOURING

Price: $4,900
Engine: T-head six-cylinder
Displacement: 524.8 cubic inches (8.6 liters)
Output: 48 horsepower
Gearbox: Four-speed selective sliding gear
Production: 749

Did You Know?

After the Great Depression, Pierce-Arrow would be another of the great early American automotive names left behind. With sales plummeting to only 167 cars in 1937, the company's assets were sold at auction on the May 13, 1938. It was a Friday.

Few automakers enjoyed more favor for as long as Pierce-Arrow. By the late 1910s, the company was neck and neck with Peerless and Packard for the title of America's premier luxury carmaker. In 1918 Pierce increased its stake in the marketplace by introducing a new 825-cubic-inch (13.5-liter) dual-valve engine, thus increasing output from the same displacement inline six used the previous year. The dual-valve six was also a quieter engine, and it returned better fuel economy than its single-valve predecessor.

The Pierce-Arrow engineering department in Buffalo had spent more than five months developing the dual-valve 66. Only four prototype cars were built, at a cost of $6,000 each. The cars reportedly went to dealers as demonstrators. The Pierce 66 prototype was the first American automobile to incorporate four-wheel hydraulic brakes.

Among the interesting features of this mammoth (147 1/2-inch/3.75-m wheelbase)

tourer is Pierce-Arrow's use of an instrument cluster incorporated into the panel under the windshield—a primitive but very efficient precursor to the dashboard. The housing contains a clock; an odometer; a drum-type speedometer; oil, fuel, and amperage gauges; push buttons to activate exterior lighting, and an ignition switch. Also note the use of an integral bulb horn with the steering column and gear shift and handbrake levers mounted inside the driver's compartment. This handsome seven-passenger touring car is the only remaining example of the Model 66 prototypes. It can be seen on exhibit at the world-famous Nethercutt Automobile Collection in Sylmar, California.

1918 PIERCE-ARROW MODEL 66 (PROTOTYPE) TOURING

Price: $6,000
Engine: Inline T-head dual-valve six-cylinder
Displacement: 824.7 cubic inches (13.5 liters)
Output: 66 horsepower
Gearbox: Four-speed selective sliding gear
Production: 4

Did You Know?

The Model 66 dual-valve prototype might be considered the first "concept car" in America. In 1918 it was the most advanced design in Pierce-Arrow's history up to that time. Many of the features developed for the prototype (as opposed to the production-line Model 66 dating to 1910) were used in post–World War I Pierce-Arrow models.

CHAPTER 3
THE CONVERTIBLE COMES OF AGE— 1921 TO 1925

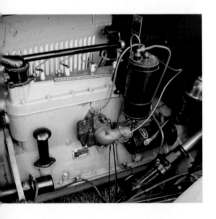

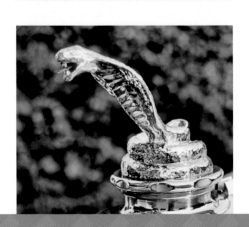

It wasn't until the early 1920s that automakers really began styling their cars. It had taken the failure of Lincoln in 1922 to really shake things up. Prior to Henry Ford purchasing the struggling Lincoln Automobile Company from founder Henry Leland, Lincoln had been an independent marque. The failure rested at Leland's feet. He was an engineer not a stylist, and like so many automakers in the first 20 years of the twentieth century, he saw styling as a function of engineering—a hood to cover the engine, fenders to cover the wheels, a body to surround the passengers, and a fabric top overhead to protect them from the elements. With few exceptions, little separated makes and models aside from grilles and radiator mascots. Automotive design had yet to become an art.

By the early 1920s, American automakers were beginning to discover what the Europeans already knew: that a few adjustments to a fender or body panel here, a little decorative brightwork there, and a greater choice in styles meant more customers and more sales—and above all, brand loyalty that was based upon more than building a solid, reliable engine and driveline. The era of the automotive stylist was about to come into its own.

Indianapolis manufacturer Nordyke and Marmon was among the most distinguished automakers of the early twentieth century, renowned for its innovative designs. The most significant Marmon of the early 1900s was the Model 34, introduced in 1916, which was followed by the further improved post–World War I Model 34B in 1920, the car acclaimed by many as Marmon's greatest. The Marmon design incorporated running boards, their supporting members, and splash pans into the load-bearing structure. While the bare chassis was somewhat unusual in appearance, it proved to be a breakthrough in platform design, achieving both a reduction in weight and an increase in strength.

1921 MARMON MODEL 34B WASP SPEEDSTER

Price: $5,300

Engine: Aluminum inline six-cylinder; overhead valve design

Displacement: 339.6 cubic inches (5.5 liters)

Output: 34 horsepower

Gearbox: Three-speed selective sliding gear

Production: N/A

The advanced design featured what Marmon called "unification construction," making the body and chassis nearly one—essentially an early version of unibody construction, which

would not become an industry standard for decades. Regarded as one of the best-handling cars on the road, the Model 34B had an even 50-50 front-to-rear weight distribution.

Marmon offered a variety of body styles with the very popular Model 34B Speedsters. These were manufactured by the Hume Body Company of Rochester, New York, and made entirely of lightweight aluminum over a braced framework of ash. The total weight of the Speedster was a mere 3,295 pounds (1,495 kg).

Noted for its distinctive "bee-back" appearance and exceptional speed—quick enough, in fact, that it could indeed have been a race car—a Marmon 34B Speedster, fitted with a special 3.0:1 ratio axle, was timed around the 2.5-mile (4-km) Indianapolis Motor Speedway at two minutes six seconds, an average of 71 miles per hour (114 km/hr), for 1920 an exceptional top speed for anything that wasn't there to race. That same year, the Speedster was chosen as the official pacesetter for the eighth running of the Memorial Day classic, with the legendary Barney Oldfield behind the wheel. To everyone's amazement, Oldfield led the starting grid around Indy at a sensational 80-mile-per-hour (129 km/hr) clip before pulling off at the end of the pace lap. Even Oldfield's celebrated rival, race driver Ralph DePalma, who was on the pole that year, remarked that the Marmon may have been the fastest car on the track!

Did You Know?

A Marmon won the first Indianapolis 500 in 1911. In 1920 Barney Oldfield was so impressed with the Marmon pacesetter's performance that he purchased the car after the race and drove it coast to coast eight times to promote a line of tires bearing his name. His cross-country trips made the car so popular with the public that on August 20, 1920, Marmon announced production of a 1921 Wasp Speedster in Marmon Racing Yellow, equipped with the special 3.0:1 axle (3.75:1 was standard) and a 0- to 100-mile-per-hour speedometer. Identical to the car driven by Oldfield, the 1921 models represent the first actual incident of a manufacturer offering replicas of an Indianapolis 500 pace car!

Although considered to be French cars, the Hispano-Suiza marque was of Spanish origin, originally founded in Barcelona by Spanish artillery major Emilio de la Cuadra. The confusion over the company's heritage stems from the 1900 opening of a new Paris factory, from which all the great designs to bear the Hispano-Suiza name and flying stork mascot would begin to appear after 1919. The mastermind of Hispano-Suiza was Swiss engineer Marc Birkigt, who created the most renowned series of cars in the company's history, the H6.

Considered the best-built automobile in Europe and priced several thousand dollars more than a Rolls-Royce, the Hispano-Suiza was regarded

1923 HISPANO-SUIZA H6B CABRIOLET

Price: $15,000

Engine: Six-cylinder; single overhead cam

Displacement: 479 cubic inches (7.8 liters)

Output: 32 horsepower

Gearbox: Three-speed manual

Production: N/A

with the highest esteem by everyone from General Motors' chief stylist Harley Earl, (who copied Hispano-Suiza styling for the 1927 LaSalle,

right down to a version of the flying stork hood ornament) to the Rothschild family, artist Pablo Picasso, and many others.

In 1923 Paris *carrossier* Jacques Saoutchik crafted the Cabriolet DeVille body for this majestic 1922 H6B. Known for his superb sense of style, tempered with just a hint of extravagance, Saoutchik was always a little ahead of his time, and in 1923 this spicy brown Hispano-Suiza was *nouvelle vague* compared to the starched-collar coachwork still befitting formal livery. The gently curving hood and cowl design and the sweeping fenders with recessed spare forecast a look that would not generally be seen until the late 1920s.

Originally selling for $15,000, the car was equipped with a removable leather cover over the chauffeur's compartment, a complicated but manageable folding rear roof section with removable "B" pillars, and luxurious leather-upholstered seating throughout. Stretching over 20 feet (6 m) in length, the Hispano's massive 479-cubic-inch (7.8-liter) six-cylinder engine could easily take the regal Cabriolet to speeds in excess of 70 miles per hour (112.6 km/hr). One of the finest examples of the marque in the world, this 1923 H6B is one of the centerpiece exhibits in the renowned Nethercutt Automobile Collection in Sylmar, California.

Did You Know?

During the First World War, Hispano-Suiza produced thousands of aero engines for the French and Allied flying squads. The famous Hispano flying stork hood ornament was the symbol of the Spad fighter squadron of French captain Georges Guynemer during the war and was adopted by the company in 1919.

It's a pity that the Kissel "Gold Bug" Speedster wasn't introduced in 1925; it would have made the ethereal cut as an American Classic, a distinction granted to only the best cars built in and after 1925 and before 1948 by those who appointed themselves the board of adjudicators (a club) after World War II to determine which American and European cars were worthy of being anointed with the title "Classic." More than half a century later, the jury is still out on a lot of those decisions, but Kissels built after 1925 are regarded as "Classic Cars."

The Kissel utilized a double drop frame to allow lower body height and thus a lower center of gravity for better handling; it was the first automobile to use

1923 KISSEL "GOLD BUG" SPEEDSTER

Price: N/A
Engine: L-head inline six-cylinder
Displacement: 265 cubic inches (4.3 liters)
Output: 32.6 horsepower
Gearbox: Three-speed manual
Production: N/A

dashboard illumination for night driving; and Kissel pioneered the use of window regulators (a precursor to roll-up windows). In addition to its sporty coachwork, accented by the conspicuous absence of running

boards (which simply wasn't done at the time), narrow-cut down doors, and beetle-back deck lid, the two-seat roadster offered one other uncommon feature: unique outrigger seats that folded neatly into compartments on either side of the body so that two more could enjoy the thrill of racing down the wind in a Kissel Speedster. This design would probably be a hard sell with today's National Highway Traffic Safety Administration, but in the 1920s it was an attractive if not daring feature.

The KisselKar Company lived a short but productive life from 1907 until 1931, a mere 24 years, during which the Hartford, Wisconsin, automaker produced what could be regarded as very modern automobiles. Following World War I, the company changed its name from KisselKar to just Kissel, fearing that the old name sounded too German (American sentiments toward Germany were still prickly in 1920). The Gold Bug was powered by an L-head six-cylinder engine of Kissel's own design, which would remain in production with only minor changes from 1915 to 1928. Among the various models manufactured, the Gold Bug became a favorite among Hollywood film stars.

Did You Know?

Cars acquire names in many ways. Today, most names are created by advertising agencies and corporate focus groups, but back in the glorious 1920s, automakers were a bit more enterprising. The Wisconsin car company publicly displayed the new Kissel model and then had a "name the car" contest. Gold Bug was chosen from out of 500 written entries.

There are many words used today to describe star power. In the 1920s, there was just one: "Valentino." When Rudolph Valentino appeared in public, women swooned, men bristled, and cameras flashed. He was a legend, and all that he touched, all that he possessed, became legend as well. A silver screen icon of the 1920s, he lived a fast life and a relatively short one, dying at age 31. Though acting was his first love, his passion was automobiles, and in the 1920s his favorite car of the many he owned was a 1923 Avions Voisin that he had had built to his specifications in France by Paris *carrossier* J. Rothschild et Fils.

1923 AVIONS VOISIN C5 SPORTING VICTORIA

Price: $14,000
Engine: Four-cylinder sleeve valve
Displacement: 3.969cc (242 cubic inches)
Output: 90 horsepower
Gearbox: Four-speed manual
Production: N/A

It took a year before he was able to take delivery of the custom-bodied Voisin C5, which cost a staggering $14,000.

The Valentino Voisin was unique in several respects; its body was designed to allow it to be configured to suit Valentino's mood and the purpose of each drive. A three-position top allowed for a fully concealed front and rear compartment, an open driver's compartment, or open touring, with the fabric completely lowered. The car also had a folding rear windscreen for more formal occasions, giving it the appearance of a dual windshield phaeton. Most often, it was driven with the top down, and by Valentino alone.

The C5 Voisin was an uncommon car, even in France. It was the product of Gabriel Voisin, who had built airplanes from the turn of the century through World War I and even claimed to have built a practical airplane before the Wright brothers. When the aircraft business dried up in the post–World War I recession, Voisin decided to build automobiles. With a huge factory and 2,000 employees at his disposal, he not only designed and built his own chassis, he produced the engines as well, working from the design of an almost unbreakable 4-liter sleeve valve four with aluminum pistons (used by Voisin throughout the 1920s) that delivered a robust 90 horsepower and a top speed of 80 miles per hour (129 km/hr).

Did You Know?

Although the Voisin had a rather stylish aluminum bird sculpture hood ornament designed by the factory, Rudolph Valentino's close actor friends Douglas Fairbanks and Mary Pickford presented him with a special silver-plated coiled hooded cobra to place atop the Voisin's radiator. The mascot was a gift following the release of Valentino's film *Cobra*.

Getting all steamed up had another meaning in the early twentieth century. Steam was one of the most popular power sources for early American automobiles, and the most advanced and expensive steam car of the era was the sporty Doble.

Scions of a wealthy industrial family, the Doble brothers had been fascinated with steam power since their early childhood. While attending the Massachusetts Institute of Technology in 1910, Abner Doble visited the Stanley brothers in Newton, Massachusetts, where he became further intrigued by the idea, taking the Stanleys' design and improving upon it through the use of a condenser that recycled exhaust steam back into the engine.

1925 DOBLE SERIES E ROADSTER

Price: As much as $11,200
Engine: Steam compound four-cylinder
Displacement: 214.14x2 cubic inches
Output: 150 horsepower
Gearbox: None
Production: Fewer than 35

Launched in 1916, the new models were so advanced in design that they required no more preparation to start than a conventional gasoline engine automobile. In just 90 seconds, a Doble had a full head of steam and was ready to roll. (A

Stanley required 20 minutes.) Once underway the Doble was almost silent until the boiler kicked in to produce additional steam, unleashing a thundering roar similar to a small jet engine. The operation of the Doble required deft attention to pressure and a keen eye on the road, as the application of brakes had to be timed with cutting back the flow of steam via a regulator lever on the steering wheel hub. There was no floor throttle and no transmission, only a foot brake, a lever to change from forward to reverse, and another regulating output from the four-cylinder engine—a staggering 150 horsepower and 1,000 lbs-ft of torque delivered at only 1 rpm!

The Doble steam engine is a compounded design, with a double bore of 2.625 and 4.500 inches and a stroke of 5.000 inches, for a cubic inch displacement of 214.14x2 cubic inches.

The average Doble measured 150 inches (3.81 m) between the axles and weighed nearly three tons, yet were it not for the complexity of the design and its sheer cost—as much as $11,200 in 1925—the mighty steam car might well have succeeded long into the 1930s. Unfortunately, Doble ran out of steam, figuratively speaking, in 1931. The Doble brothers, in their new Emeryville, California, facility, produced fewer than 30 cars in the E and later F series and never made a profit.

Did You Know?

The Walter M. Murphy Company of Pasadena, California, one of the leading coachbuilders in America during the 1920s and early 1930s, built this beautiful Doble Series E-20 roadster for millionaire industrialist and filmmaker Howard Hughes. The handsome coachwork has a completely disappearing convertible top, a specially modified engine with higher steam pressure (2000 psi), ordered by Hughes, and a 1:1 ring and pinion. As equipped for Hughes, the Doble could attain a top speed of 133 miles per hour (214 km/hr)! The car can be seen today at the Nethercutt Museum in Sylmar, California.

CHAPTER 4
CLASSIC AMERICAN CONVERTIBLES— 1926 TO 1941

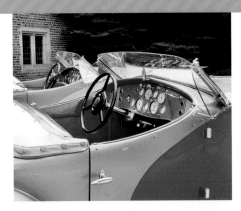

What is a Classic Car? The term has been so abused over the years that it now applies to almost anything built in the last century. But in point of fact, nothing built after 1948 is a Classic Car. *Nothing*. A 1957 Thunderbird is a great looking car, but it's not a Classic. In fact, only a handful of American cars produced between 1925 and 1948 have ever been accorded Classic status, and those that have are regarded as the greatest automobiles of their time, perhaps of any time. The majority were built during what was perhaps the worst possible period in America's early–twentieth-century history, at the height of the Great Depression. With the nation's economy in shambles, the country's leading automakers were just hitting their creative stride by the 1930s.

The 1930s couldn't have been a worse time for most of what transpired in the automotive industry. It started the first January after the great Wall Street Crash of 1929 with Cadillac unveiling a 16-cylinder luxury car. Shortly after the Cadillac's debut, Marmon introduced a V-16. That was one more sixteen than the marketplace could sustain. Marmon was the first of the great American names to fall by the side of the road during the years of the Great Depression. While no one else wanted to challenge Cadillac for the most cylinders under one hood, the GM luxury division had also thrown down a second gauntlet by introducing a V-12, and that was a challenge that Lincoln, Packard, Pierce-Arrow, and others couldn't resist. Thus in the middle of a financial meltdown, America's top automakers began building the most powerful and luxurious, and yes, expensive, automobiles of the early 20th century.

It had begun in December 1928, less than a year before the stock market crash, with the introduction of the Model J Duesenberg. This was to become the quintessential American Classic. The Duesenberg's straight-eight engine developed exceptional power for its time: 265 horsepower in standard trim and a staggering 320 horsepower when equipped with a supercharged SJ engine, added in 1932.

The Model J engine and chassis, designed by Fred Duesenberg, was of unrivaled strength, endowing the cars with superior handling and performance. And every one of the approximately 485 examples

1936 DUESENBERG MODEL J, SJ, AND SSJ

Price: $8,500 for bare running chassis complete with grille, fenders, running boards, hood, cowl, steering wheel, and instrument panel. Coachwork was extra.

Engine: Straight-eight dual overhead cam

Displacement: 420 cubic inches (6.88 liters)

Output: 265 horsepower (normally aspirated) or 320 horsepower (supercharged)

Gearbox: Three-speed selective gear

Production: Approximately 485 (all J, SJ, and SSJ chassis)

built between 1928 and 1937, when E. L. Cord's Auburn, Cord, Duesenberg automotive empire collapsed, were fitted with handmade, coachbuilt bodies of extraordinary quality and cost. In the 1930s, a coachbuilt Model J averaged $15,000, making it the most expensive American car on the road. Even Cadillac's great V-16 All-Weather Phaeton commanded only $7,350, and the popular V-16 Sport Phaeton cost $6,500, which was $2,000 *less* for an entire car than a Model J chassis cost in 1930!

The sporty Duesenberg speedsters and convertibles were the super sports cars of their time, like the Ferraris or Lamborghinis of later decades. For film stars such as Gary Cooper, Clark Gable, Carol Lombard, and James Cagney, a Duesenberg was the car in which to be seen. Gable and Cooper owned several, including the only two short wheelbase supercharged SSJ Speedsters built (shown here). Cooper's was two-tone gray, with the lighter shade running into the sweep panel; Gable's was a warm shade of silver, with a contrasting red sweep panel.

Did You Know?

The mechanical design of the Duesenberg Model J straight-eight engine used dual overhead cams and four valves per cylinder, features still used in today's high-performance cars. A Duesenberg race car won the 24 Hours of Le Mans in 1921 and the Indianapolis 500 in 1924. The triumphant Indy racer was powered by a supercharged straight eight. In 1935 a Duesenberg SJ driven by Ab Jenkins set a land speed record of 152.145 miles per hour (244.853 km/hr) at the Bonneville Salt Flats.

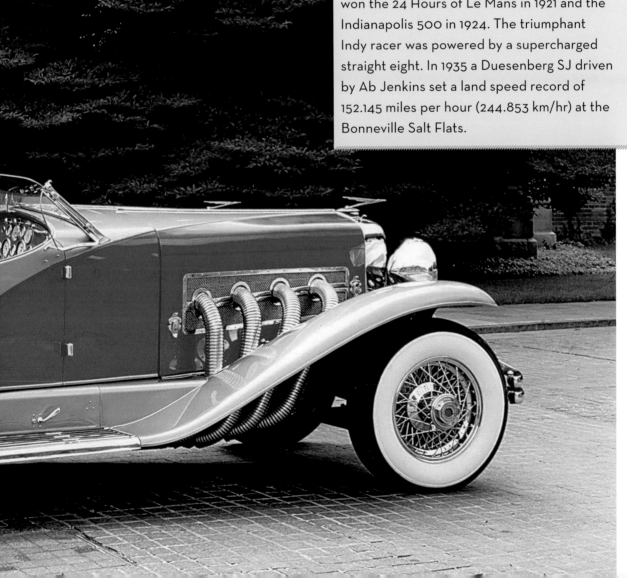

1936 DUESENBERG MODEL J, SJ, AND SSJ

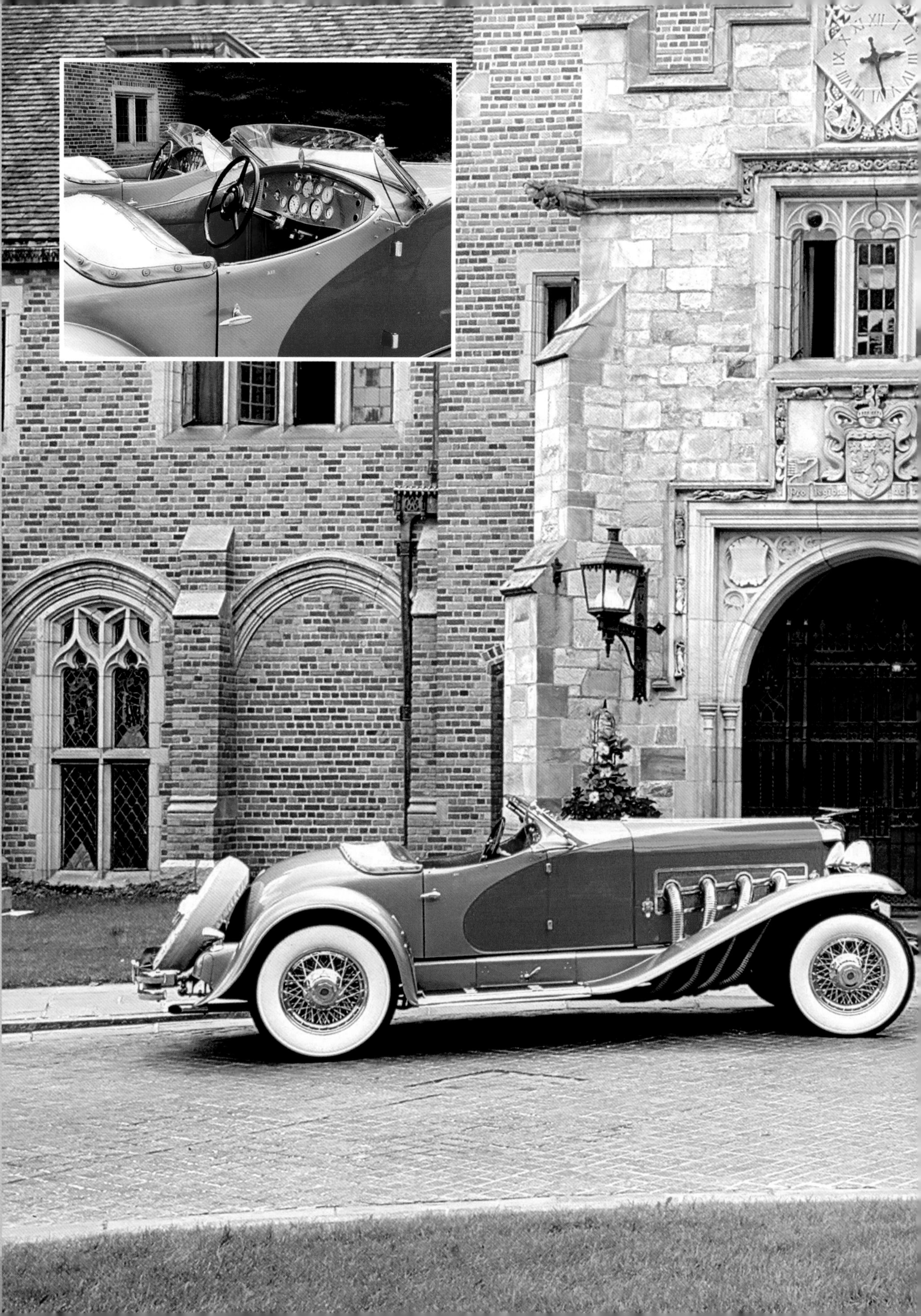

Late in 1929, everything was being readied at Cadillac for the introduction of the most ostentatious automobile America had ever seen. Then came Black Tuesday: October 29, 1929. Between Thursday October 24 and Tuesday October 29, a record number of shares changed hands on Wall Street, and investors started a sell-off that sent the New York Stock Exchange into free fall, resulting in listed equities losing more than $26 billion in value. The world was about to plummet into the worst economic catastrophe of the twentieth century just as Cadillac prepared to unveil the most expensive car in its history, the V-16.

1930 CADILLAC V-16

Price: $6,500 (Dual Windshield Sport Phaeton)
Engine: V-16
Displacement: 452 cubic inches (7.4 liters)
Output: 185 horsepower
Gearbox: Three speed
Production: 85

On January 4, 1930, the effects of the stock market crash hadn't yet been realized, and at the annual New York Automobile Show, held at the fashionable Waldorf Astoria Hotel, Cadillac formally introduced

its all-new sixteen-cylinder model. The engine was basically two inline eights sharing a common crankshaft. The cylinder banks were placed at a very narrow 45-degree angle, and each had its own independent fuel and exhaust system. The V-16 used overhead valves, a design not previously seen on a Cadillac, and hydraulic valve adjustment, an industry first, which contributed to the Cadillac's exceptionally smooth and near-silent operation. Not as fleet of foot as the eight-cylinder Duesenberg, a Cadillac could attain a top speed of 100 miles per hour (161 km/hr) when fitted with lighter coachwork, like a roadster or a convertible coupe. Most, however, never surpassed 80 miles per hour (129 km/hr) on the open road.

Dazzling Fleetwood designs such as the Dual Windshield Sport Phaeton (the red model shown here) featured a roll-up rear divider windshield and an elegant burled and ebony wood instrument fascia built into the front seat back, providing rear occupants with a speedometer and Jaeger chronometer. Up front, there was comfortable seating for two and an ornate instrument panel with gauges surrounded by an elaborate crosshatch-pattern steel fascia, flanked by a polished, damascened dashboard. Built on a 148-inch (3.75-m) wheelbase chassis and stretching nearly 20 feet (6 m) in length, only 85 Dual Windshield Sport Phaetons were produced. With a cataloged price of $6,500, it was right in the middle of the V-16 lineup.

Did You Know?
The majority of Cadillac V-16s were limousines, town cars, and formal sedans. However, about four out of five chassis went on to become sporty open cars such as the Fleetwood-bodied Dual Windshield Sport Phaeton, and these have become the most prized of the 16-cylinder models. The Cadillac V-16 also had the first automobile engine anywhere to bear the mark of a stylist. It was a striking combination of bright chrome, polished aluminum, black porcelain, and gleaming enamel, with as much wiring as possible discretely hidden from view.

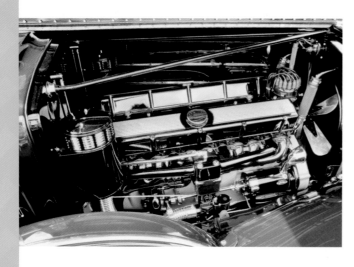

Occasionally, a model name will acquire significance as great as the company that created it, becoming so well recognized that car and carmaker become synonymous. Examples include Corvette and Chevrolet, and 911 and Porsche. The same distinction applies to Imperial, a name linked with the Chrysler Corporation since 1926, the year Walter P. Chrysler introduced the new luxury model at New York City's National Automobile Show.

The Imperial line consisted of a roadster, a coupe, a phaeton, five- and seven-passenger sedans, and a seven-passenger limousine. A custom-bodied landaulet and town car were also available on the

1931 CHRYSLER CG IMPERIAL 8 ROADSTER

Price: $3,220
Engine: "Red Head" straight eight
Displacement: 385 cubic inches (6.3 liters)
Output: 125 horsepower
Gearbox: Four-speed manual
Production: 100

Imperial's 127- and 133-inch (3.22- and 3.37-m) wheelbase chassis. In 1926 Chrysler received the greatest endorsement any automaker could hope

for when an Imperial roadster was chosen as the official pace car for the 145th Indianapolis 500.

Imperials were ranked among the best-engineered and best-built automobiles in America—the equal of Cadillac, Lincoln, and Packard in terms of status. Among the most stylish was the 1931 CG Imperial 8 Roadster, powered by Chrysler's famous "Red Head" straight eight that delivered 125 horsepower.

While the average man desiring a sporty, distinctive car may have worked long and hard to purchase a 1931 Ford Deluxe Roadster (Ford sold more than 53,000 in 1931, at a starting price of just $475), he would have had to work a lot harder to buy a Chrysler CG Imperial 8 Roadster, priced at $3,220. Only 100 were sold in 1931.

Did You Know?

The front end of the LeBaron-designed Chryslers look suspiciously similar to the popular Cord L-29; both cars sport sharply pointed V-type radiator shells; broad, sweeping fenders; sloping, split windshields; and extremely long hoods. The long hood design, created by LeBaron's Ralph Roberts, was originally rejected by Edsel Ford for the 1932 Lincoln line. When Walter Chrysler saw it, he said to Roberts, "Can't we have that? That long, long hood is really something." It became a standard Chrysler styling cue in 1932.

Lincoln was Edsel Ford's domain, his sanctuary away from a despotic and overbearing father. Not exactly the image one pictures of Henry Ford, but the elder Ford was disposed to management by intimidation, and lacking Edsel's creative eye, the father was always in conflict with his son over how Ford Motor Company's luxury car division should be run.

Although Cadillac and Packard virtually owned the prestige name in America of the 1930s, Lincolns were generally perceived as the best engineered, most mechanically reliable, and most attractive cars of the era. This was, for the most part, due to Edsel Ford, whose exceptional sense of style had guided the company's selection of coachwork and coachbuilders since the Ford Motor Company had made an $8

1932 LINCOLN KB DUAL COWL SPORT PHAETON

Price: $3,220
Engine: V-12
Displacement: 447.9 cubic inches (7.3 liters)
Output: 150 horsepower
Gearbox: Three-speed manual with integral free wheeling
Production: 43

million investment to purchase Lincoln from Henry and Wilfred Leland in 1922.

In 1932 Lincoln introduced the all-new KB line, powered by one of the most powerful engines on the market, a 447.9-cubic-inch (7.3-l) V-12 that tipped the scales at more than half a

ton and delivered 150 horsepower. As the new flagship of Lincoln, the KB was available in more than 25 different body styles, the most classic being the Murphy-bodied Dual Cowl Sport Phaeton. The sporty four-passenger model was upholstered in hand-buffed leather, available in brown or black finish, and could be ordered either with or without the rear cowl. Lincoln used the dual cowl design pioneered by LeBaron, wherein the rear panel released when the doors opened and tilted up out of the way. The Lincoln KB Dual Cowl Sport Phaeton was originally offered by the factory, but the majority of bodies were produced by the Walter M. Murphy Company in Pasadena, California. Only 43 were built—consummate examples of the magnificent classic-era Lincolns.

Did You Know?

The secret to Lincoln's success under Ford was in the coachwork. Edsel was a stylist at heart and even selected the graceful greyhound mascot for Lincoln, which was produced for Ford by Gorham. Some say the takeover of Lincoln in 1922 by the Ford Motor Company, and the ousting of Henry Leland, was just desserts. Back in 1902, Henry Ford had been forced to resign from his original company (the Henry Ford Company, established in October 1901) after investors lost faith and brought in a consultant named Henry Leland, who took over the company and turned it into Cadillac at the end of 1902.

1932 LINCOLN KB DUAL COWL SPORT PHAETON

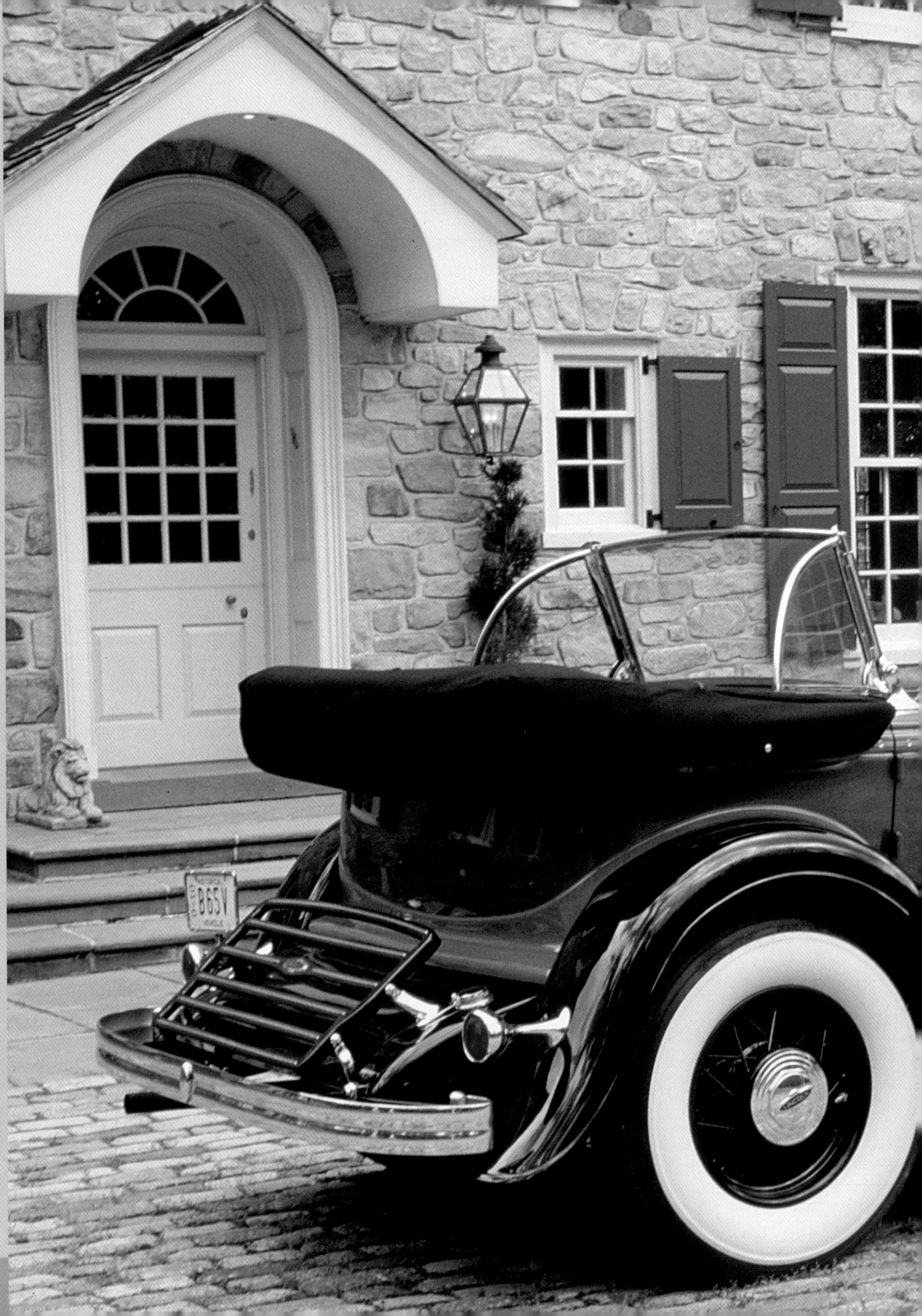

Under the guidance of Errett Lobban Cord, the Auburn Automobile Company prospered throughout the late 1920s. The company had passed an annual sales goal of 20,000 cars by the time the New York Stock Exchange plunged over the edge in October 1929. In spite of the deepening depression, Auburn production soared to a record 32,301 units in 1931, the result of Cord's dealer expansion program, plus an all-eight-cylinder line of beautiful, luxurious, and bargain-priced models. Unfortunately, as the 1930s wore on, the economy failed to rebound as most had expected, and Auburn sales began to plunge. In a last-ditch

1935 AUBURN 851 BOATTAIL SPEEDSTER

Price: $2,245
Engine: Supercharged Lycoming straight eight
Displacement: 279.2 cubic inches (4.57 liters)
Output: 150 horsepower
Gearbox: Three-speed manual
Production: 500

effort to reignite the company, E. L. Cord made a bold—some might call foolhardy—move in 1934, spending $500,000 to redesign the entire Auburn

model line. When the new models failed to increase sales, Duesenberg's chief designer, Gordon Miller Buehrig, was given a modest $50,000 and told to do what he could to upgrade Auburn styling once more for 1935. Augie Duesenberg was handed the 1935 engine assignment, in conjunction with Schwitzer-Cummins and Lycoming, which yielded a new supercharged 279.2-cubic-inch (4.57-liters) eight-cylinder engine developing 150 horsepower. The new 1935 lineup was introduced in June 1934.

Despite what could only be deemed a dazzling selection of cars, cabriolets, broughams, phaetons, sedans, and the stunning 851 Boattail Speedster, Auburn had sold only 7,000 cars by 1936. The Auburn 851 was sporty, boldly styled with four exhaust pipes cascading out of the left hood side panel. There was just a hint of a cockpit, resembling an airplane's more than an automobile's, with the remainder of the body consumed by a sleek, tapered "boattail" and pontoon fenders. The most flamboyant American car of its time, a virtual icon for speed, it was everything but Auburn's savior. A total of 500 were built between 1935 and 1936. Alas, the 1937 Speedsters never arrived. Nor did any other Auburn model.

Did You Know?

The 851 Boattail Speedster became the most famous Auburn model ever built, a car with all the character and vitality of a Duesenberg at a fraction of the price. It was fast—guaranteed to exceed 100 miles per hour (161 km/hr). A plaque on the dashboard read: "This certifies that this Auburn automobile has been driven 100.8 miles per hour before shipment." It was signed by world-renowned land-speed record holder Ab Jenkins.

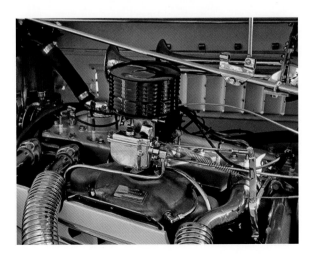

1935 AUBURN 851 BOATTAIL SPEEDSTER

CHAPTER 5
GREAT EUROPEAN DROPHEAD COUPES AND CABRIOLETS

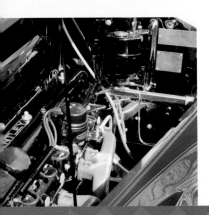

Every great car built during the classic era of the 1930s and 1940s was actually comprised of two cars—the chassis and the coachwork. Each without the other was incomplete, but a great chassis and a powerful engine clothed in an unattractive body was far worse than a mediocre chassis surrounded by exquisite coachwork by one of Europe's leading designers.

In the 1930s no country produced more exhilarating cars than France, at least as far as styling was concerned. Mercedes-Benz had Sindelfingen turning out dazzling designs like the Model S Tourer, Trossi SSK, and 540K Special Roadster; England had its legendary Bentley Drop Heads, but when it came to sheer, chest swelling enthusiasm for coachwork and avant-garde styling, there was no place like Paris, La Ville-Lumière (The City of Light) for a coachbuilt body.

In Italy, there were many automakers in the 1930s and 1940s but none more revered than Alfa Romeo, one of Italy's oldest. Following World War I, the company Alfa was merged with Nicola Romeo & Co., to become Alfa Romeo. Although Alfa Romeo built racing cars, and winning ones at that, the company's road cars are still regarded as some of the greatest ever built. Until the postwar era, Alfa Romeos were essentially hand-built automobiles produced in very limited numbers. From 1910 to 1950, only 12,200 cars were constructed; that's an average of less than one car per day! The 1930s were truly the end of an era!

For Daimler and Benz, the 1930s marked the first full decade of their amalgamation as a single company, an era highlighted by far-reaching advancements in engine, chassis, and suspension design that would put Mercedes-Benz at the forefront of the European automotive industry by 1940. However, what truly set Mercedes-Benz models apart from other cars of the era was the magnificent coachwork designed at the factory's renowned Sindelfingen Werk. Named for the city where Daimler first established a factory for aero engines and aircraft, Sindelfingen later became the *Karosserie* (body factory) for Daimler-Benz.

The master of Daimler's design and engineering department in the 1920s was Ferdinand Porsche,

1927 MERCEDES-BENZ MODEL S TOURING

Price: N/A

Engine: Supercharged straight six

Displacement: 6.79 liters (414 cubic inches)

Output: 180 horsepower with supercharger engaged

Gearbox: Four-speed manual

Production: 128

who had stepped in as chief engineer prior to the merger of Daimler and Benz in 1926. The first truly great car to bear the Porsche signature was the Model S, introduced in 1927. The Model S (and subsequent

SS and SSK, designed by Porsche's successor, Dr. Hans Nibel) was built on a new drop-center frame with a 133-inch (3.37-m) standard wheelbase. To improve handling over earlier Mercedes, Porsche moved the radiator and engine about a foot rearward on the chassis, resulting in better front-to-rear weight distribution and a lower center of gravity. The lower chassis also improved cornering and encouraged more rakish, open coachwork.

With the improved chassis also came greater output from the Mercedes-Benz supercharged inline six: 120 horsepower under normal aspiration, 180 with the supercharger engaged. The updated engine in the Model S had its bore increased from 94mm (3.70 inches) to 98mm (3.85 inches). With a 150mm (5.90-inches) stroke, this brought displacement up to 6,789cc (about 414 cubic inches). Production of the supercharged S or Sport (180-horsepower) model was limited to 128 chassis.

Off the track, nearly all Model S body styles were of the open touring design, but they were very traditional, severe, and upright in appearance. The majority of bodies were designed and manufactured by the Sindelfingen Werk, but S Series chassis were also fitted with coachwork designed in Germany by Karosserie Erdmann & Rossi or Karosserie Papler, and in Geneva, Switzerland, by Zeitz, which created the body for the Model S Touring pictured.

Did You Know?

Racing versions of the production Model S, SS, and SSK, equipped with higher-compression engines, ran on Elcosine, an alcohol-fuel mixture used for competition, and were capable of speeds well in excess of 100 miles per hour (161 km/hr). In one of these competition versions, Rudolf Caracciola surpassed 120 miles per hour (193 km/hr).

Of the 33 Mercedes-Benz SSK models produced, the most famous and perhaps most magnificently styled was a car built for Count Carlo Felice "Didi" Trossi. An Italian aristocrat whose family lineage dated back to the 14th century, Trossi was a proficient race driver and president of Scuderia Ferrari (the Alfa Romeo race team) in the early 1930s. In 1933 Trossi won some minor Italian events, but whether or not he drove the sleek SSK in competition is not documented. In 1934 he entered Grand Prix racing and twice finished second to the legendary Tazio Nuvolari! By the end of the 1930s, he was one of the top drivers in Italy, and after the war he raced for Alfa Romeo. In 1947 he won the

1930 TROSSI MERCEDES-BENZ SSK

Engine: Supercharged straight six
Displacement: 7.1 liters (433.2 cubic inches)
Output: 300 horsepower with supercharger engaged
Gearbox: Four-speed manual
Production: 33 (SSK chassis)

Italian GP, and won the European GP the following year, ended the season as European Champion. During his career he finished in the top three places some 40 times. Trossi died of cancer in 1949 at the age of 41.

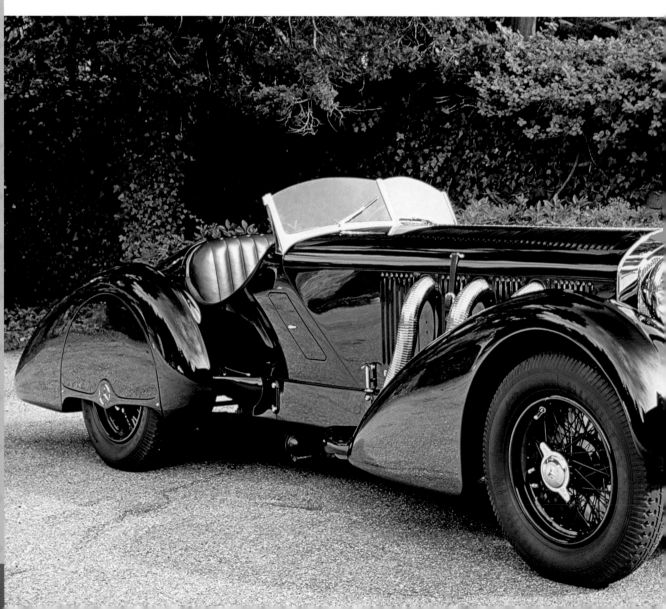

Built in 1932–1933 on a 1930 SSK chassis, the body was handcrafted in England, purportedly from Trossi's own design drawings. The design of the cockpit in Trossi's car was reminiscent of several fighter planes of the era—not surprising, as Trossi was also an accomplished pilot. Under the sleek hood of the Trossi SSK was the mighty Mercedes straight-six-cylinder, supercharged engine designed by Porsche. The trio of polished exhausts was symbolic as well as functional. The output of the 7.1-liter (433.2-cubic-inch) engine in Trossi's car was 300 horsepower at 3,400 rpm! The Trossi SSK is now part of the Ralph Lauren Collection.

Did You Know?

With its avant-garde styling, the Trossi SSK was unlike any other car of the early 1930s. It is hard to believe that this sporty two-seater, with a 116-inch (2.94-m) wheelbase, had a longer platform than a 2011 E-Class wagon! This SSK is one of the few cars in history ever to become known by its original owner's surname.

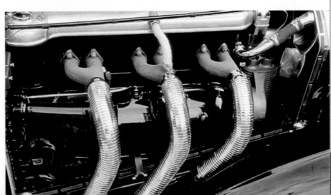

French coachwork had developed into a true art form by the 1930s, and the masters of the French design idiom were Joseph Figoni, Henri Chapron, and Jacques Saoutchik. All three were fascinated with aerodynamics and were continually searching for ways to cheat the wind. Figoni pioneered a body style called Goutte d'eau, which literally translated means "teardrop" or "raindrop," nature's perfect aerodynamic shape. This shape was the inspiration for nearly all the unorthodox yet hauntingly beautiful designs that came out of France in the 1930s—cars resplendent in long, skirted fenders, sweptback hood lines, and tapered tails. The very best bore a single name, Bugatti.

1939 BUGATTI TYPE 57C

Price: N/A

Engine: Third version, supercharged (C compressor) straight eight

Displacement: 3257cc

Output: 200 horsepower with supercharger engaged

Gearbox: Four-speed manual or optional Cotal electro-mechanical gearbox

Production: 670 (includes all the 57s produced)

Ettore Bugatti's factory at Molsheim, in Alsace, an occasionally disputed border region between France and Germany, was the source of what many

collectors of rolling antiquity consider to be the greatest sporting automobiles of the 1920s and 1930s. The factory was run by Ettore and later by his son Jean, one of the most brilliant automotive designers of the 1930s. From the time he was 20, the styling studio had been Jean's domain, and his designs, though often controversial, were the most stirring to ever grace a French automobile chassis.

During his tenure as acting director, Jean embarked upon the design of a single production model capable of bearing a variety of body styles, a car bred from Bugatti racing heritage but refined for the open road. The result was the Type 57, the most celebrated nonracing Bugatti ever produced.

From the car's introduction in 1934 to the assembly of the last models early in 1940, a total of 670 Type 57, 57S, 57C, and 57SC versions were manufactured, more than any other Bugatti. The original 3.3-liter (201-cubic-inch) straight eight used in the Type 57 employed a six-main bearing crankshaft, integral head and block, and two valves per cylinder actuated by Miller-inspired dual overhead camshafts; output from the early engines was 135 horsepower. The supercharged 57C version shown here—with coachwork by Jacques Saoutchik—produced 200 horsepower.

Did You Know?

The Type 57 was the first Bugatti to integrate the gearbox with the engine, using a single dry-plate clutch. The cars could be ordered with the Cotal electromechanical preselect gearbox favored by race drivers. Utilizing a miniaturized gearbox mounted on the steering column, the driver could preset a lower or higher gear with the touch of a finger and engage it at will by tapping the clutch pedal. The stunning coachwork on this black 1939 Bugatti 57C Roadster was created by Jacques Saoutchik and is believed to be the only two-passenger Type 57C designed by the renowned French automotive stylist.

The European tradition of beautiful coachbuilt cars barely survived the horrors of World War II. The art, however, was not altogether lost in postwar France, where it remained in the hands of a few stalwart individuals whose firms had survived—Henri Chapron, Jacques Saoutchik, Joseph Figoni, and the Franay brothers. The Franays' survival was doubtlessly aided by the select clientele they had served before the war. Among the notables who patronized their salon postconflict were General Charles de Gaulle, England's Edward VIII, Prince Nicholas of Romania, the king of Sweden, numerous maharajahs, French nobility, and even a Vanderbilt.

In 1947 A. J. Liechti commissioned this Mk VI Bentley with coachwork crafted by Franay. Liechti,

1947 BENTLEY MK VI FRANAY CABRIOLET

Price: N/A

Engine: Cast-iron inline six

Displacement: 4.257 liters (259.9 cubic inches)

Output: 100–125 horsepower at 3,750 rpm

Gearbox: Four-speed manual

Production: 5,201 (Mark VI chassis, 1946–1952)

of the wealthy Basel, Switzerland–based J. G. Liechti family, wanted his cabriolet built on the finest chassis available, which in his estimation was the Mk VI Bentley. The lighter and better-balanced Mk VI chassis was a masterpiece, the best Bentley ever,

although probably not in the eyes of W. O. Bentley purists, who staunchly hold to the belief that the marque literally died in 1931 upon its acquisition by Rolls-Royce. (It is doubtful they feel any better today, with Rolls-Royce and Bentley independent of each other and both owned by German automakers!) Nevertheless, the Mk VI offered performance, ride, and handling characteristics that made it unique in its time. It was the equal of or superior to any other motorcar built in Europe, or the world for that matter.

The Mk VI was produced from 1946 through 1952, when it was replaced by the all-new R types. In total, 5,201 chassis were built, and all but 999 were fitted with standard coachwork. The Franay Bentley drophead, mounted on Mk VI chassis B26BH,

was a simply breathtaking car with its sweeping fenders, rakish body lines, and abundant use of chrome flashing to accent the fenders. The *goutte d'eau* styling discipline gave the Bentley's fenders new prominence—the shoe wearing the foot, as it were. The high-crowned front and rear fender served to reduce air resistance. Of course, with upright radiators, freestanding headlamps, and a convertible top, most of the aerodynamic gains, if any, were for naught. *Car from the Gene and Marlene Epstein Collection.*

Did You Know?

The car seen here is one of only two 1947 Bentley Mk VI chassis bodied in Paris by Franay. Despite the aerodynamic intentions of the sleek *goutte d'eau* design idiom made fashionable in the late 1930s, the upright grille of the 1947 Bentley obstructs airflow over the body like a 4x8 sheet of plywood! The only things sweeping rearward are the wings of the Flying B mascot. Grilles notwithstanding, the advances in body design pioneered by the French design houses of the 1930s were all heading in the right direction.

725 JT 75

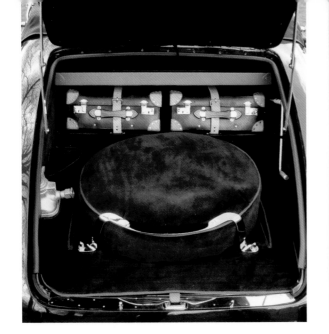

The sleek and modern envelope-bodied 1939 Alfa Romeo 6C 2500 was one of the last great prewar Italian sports cars. As one of the first European automakers to get back into production after the war ended in 1945, Alfa began by reprising the 6C 2500 models originally built from 1939 through 1941. Because the cars spanned both prewar and postwar periods, it is difficult to categorize their design as indicative of either era. It is definitely not vintage in the sense of a "1930s" Alfa Romeo, yet it is far from being a contemporary postwar car. With Solomon-like wisdom, prewar models are granted Classic Car status by the Classic Car Club of America, and postwar cars are recognized by the Milestone Car Society. For Alfa Romeo, the 6C 2500 is a unique double fait accompli in the world of collectible automobiles.

In either prewar or postwar form, like this 1947 Sport, the 6C 2500 has become one of the most desirable of Alfa Romeo models and is among the last coachbuilt production sports cars to be manufactured in Italy. This is a distinction apart from modern production sports cars, such as Ferraris, that are mass produced, albeit in handcrafted fashion. The 6C 2500 Sport (Touring) and Super Sport (with a higher-performance

engine) were fitted with cabriolet bodies hand built by Carrozzeria Pininfarina. The cabriolets were characterized by simple, uncomplicated lines and a low, wide stance, not too different from the Pininfarina-designed Cisitalia, regarded as the first modern sports car. The bumpers were almost nonexistent, leaving the tall Alfa grille unchallenged for visual impact.

The interior featured lavish appointments of rich, hand-sewn leather upholstery, plush carpeting, and a remarkable instrument panel fitted with ornate, jewel-like gauges flanked by stylish Ivorlite control knobs, resembling carved ivory.

The 6C 2500s were powered by a 2.443-liter (149-cubic-inch) six-cylinder DOHC engine with hemispheric combustion chambers. Sport models had a single two-barrel carburetor and a 7:1 compression ratio and developed 90 horsepower, while the higher performance Super Sport engine produced 105 horsepower utilizing three horizontal single-barrel carburetors and a compression of 7.5:1.

1947 ALFA ROMEO 6C 2500 SPORT

Price: N/A
Engine: DOHC inline six with hemispheric combustion chambers
Displacement: 2.443 liters (149 cubic inches)
Output: 90–105 horsepower (Sport and Super Sport)
Gearbox: Four-speed synchromesh
Production: 2,594 total 6C 2500s, 1939 to 1953; 1,140 Super Sports; 458 Sports

Did You Know?

The 6C 2500 Alfas were almost all designed to accommodate five passengers, with unique three-across front seating and two passengers cached in the narrower rear seat. The front bench was divided into a small adjustable driver's seat and a wide twin passenger seat—unusual, but far better than a traditional bench.

CHAPTER 6
POSTWAR EVOLUTION OF CONVERTIBLES— 1945 TO 1959

Sometimes the best place to begin a story is at the end. The year was 1959, and the United States was ending a decade unlike any other. So much had changed between the end of World War II and 1959 that Americans were simply awestruck. That sounds laughable today, when changes in world geopolitics and technology are so far reaching each year— sometimes each month. Nevertheless, in the 1950s, every new idea that came along, especially in the automobile industry, seemed miraculous.

The United States had been homebound since February 2, 1942, when civilian automobile production was halted. The last automobile, a Ford sedan, rolled off the River Rouge assembly line in Michigan just ahead of the first B-24 bomber. After four long years of hardship, shortages of everything from tires to engine parts, gasoline rationing, and a 35-mile-per-hour (56 km/hr) national speed limit, no wonder Americans were making substantial deposits to get on waiting lists and paying under the table to purchase new cars in 1946, even if they were only restyled 1942 models. In the few short years between 1946 and the first models of the 1950s, both the American and European automobile industries reinvented themselves. The 1950s marked the dawning of a new era, and America's love affair with automobiles was about to turn into a long-term relationship.

There is nothing like the symphony of sound that permeates the passenger compartment of a convertible: tires singing their song as they roll ribbons of pavement into fleeting images in the rearview mirror, the rush of wind surging over the windshield, the mechanical tune of the engine, and the rumble of exhaust filling the air. In the 1950s, this was driving at its absolute best, and few cars made that drive more enjoyable than a Hudson Hornet, America's leading high-performance champion. Hudson? Believe it or not, in the 1950s Hudson Hornets cleaned just about everyone's clock in AAA and NASCAR competitions!

1952 HUDSON HORNET BROUGHAM

Price: $2,500

Engine: L-head six

Displacement: 308 cubic inches (5 liters)

Output: 160 horsepower (170 with Twin-H carburetion)

Gearbox: Three-speed automatic on column

Production: Approximately 7,000 Hornet 6 Seres 7B

Hudsons were offered in four different body styles: a four-door Sedan, a two-door Club Coupe (a favorite for racing), two-door Convertible Brougham, and two-door Hollywood Hardtop.

Hornets measured 208 inches (5.28 m) from bumper to bumper on a 124-inch (3.14-m) wheelbase and tipped the scales at 3,600 pounds (1,633 kg). A 308-cubic-inch (5-l) inline six-cylinder side valve engine, drawing fuel from a Carter two-barrel carburetor, powered all four models. A Twin-H option, (twin carburetors) was added in 1952 and offered through 1954, as was a dual-range HydraMatic transmission.

From 1951 through 1953, output from the L-head six with the single Carter was a substantial 145 horsepower at 3,800 rpm, 160 horsepower with the Twin-H. This was increased to a vigorous 160 at 3,800 rpm and 170 with Twin-H in 1954, the last year for Hudson. It was a grand way to go out. On May 1, 1954, Hudson merged with Nash to form American Motors. While the merger was the road to survival for Nash, it was a dead-end street for Hudson.

Did You Know?

Every Hudson used competition-proven engineering: an A-arm and coil spring independent front suspension and rugged solid axle rear with semielliptical leaf springs, direct-acting shock absorbers at all four corners, a dual-acting front stabilizer, and a lateral stabilizer in the rear. Hudsons featured a "step-down" chassis that placed the passenger compartment within the frame members, allowing a lower roofline without sacrificing headroom. In the early 1950s, Hudsons were among the safest cars on the American road.

In 1953 General Motors made a bold and ambitious move with the debut of a "Dream Car" called the Corvette. The innovative new model was displayed at the GM Motorama in New York City. Designed by legendary stylist Harley Earl, the Corvette was a stunning concept based on sporty European two-seaters like the MG TC and Jaguar XK-120. Unfortunately, looks only went so far. Earl had incorporated the essence of the British sports cars, which Americans immediately misunderstood as cutting corners. Consumers were confounded by the features of the Corvette, or rather lack thereof, such as exterior door handles, roll-up windows, and a

1953–1955 CHEVROLET CORVETTE

Price: $3,498 (1953), $2,774 (1954–1955), $2,909 (1955 V-8)

Engine: OHV inline six or V-8

Displacement: 235 cubic inches/3.85 liters (six cylinder); 265 cubic inches/4.34 liters (V-8)

Gearbox: Two-speed automatic (1953–1954), optional three-speed manual (late 1955)

Output: 150 horsepower (six); 195 horsepower (V-8)

Production: 300 in 1953; 3,640 in 1954; 700 in 1955

weatherproof convertible top. Diehard British sports car enthusiasts understood the car's deficiencies but would have expected these to be made up for with lively performance. Unfortunately, that wasn't the case. Earl had pretty much done what he wanted when it came to body design, but Chevrolet's engineering department had to answer to a higher authority: the accountants. Budget limitations required that Chevy use an existing engine and transmission, and thus the 1953–1954 Corvette was powered by a moderately "tweaked" 150-horsepower overhead valve six-cylinder engine from the passenger car line, coupled to a two-speed automatic transmission.

Sports car enthusiasts were anything but enthusiastic for the new Chevrolet roadster. By late 1954, nearly half the cars built for the model year were collecting dust on Chevy showroom floors and dealer lots. The 300 Polo White cars built in 1953 had sold out because they were a novelty, but by 1954 the Corvette had lost its appeal to the general public.

In 1955 Chevrolet introduced a second Corvette model, this time offering it with a V-8 engine. It was the first step in redeeming the two-seat convertible among sports car cognoscente. The V-8 models were easily identified by the large gold *V* in the Chevrolet name and a lot more performance when you stepped on the throttle. The two-speed automatic was also replaced by an optional three-speed manual toward the end of 1955.

Did You Know?

GM had used fiberglass for the Motorama Corvette simply for convenience and had intended to tool up and produce the bodies in steel after a limited run of 300 special fiberglass Corvettes identical to the Motorama show car. But the public was so intrigued with fiberglass, and the fledgling plastics industry so willing to help produce the car, that Chevrolet was persuaded to continue manufacturing the bodies out of fiberglass.

1953 PENNA
59GC1

In 1953 Cadillac changed the way Americans would look at luxury cars for the rest of the century, and they did it with one word, "Eldorado." The new Cadillac had the most publicized debut in new car history; the very first one was given to President Dwight David Eisenhower for use in his inaugural parade. A classic press photograph shows Ike standing in the back of the Eldorado waving to the crowds lining Pennsylvania Avenue.

The car Ike rode in and the rest of the 1953 Eldorados were a one-year-only model. That may sound contradictory, since the Eldorado is still produced today, but the 1953 model was a special

1953 CADILLAC ELDORADO

Price: $7,750
Engine: V-8
Displacement: 331 cubic inches (5.42 liters)
Output: 210 horsepower
Gearbox: HydraMatic
Production: 532

limited edition. The following year it became a version of the Series 62 convertible, priced $2,000 less than in 1953 and built in such numbers as the market would absorb.

The 1953 Eldorado was a benchmark design, introducing innovations such as the panoramic wraparound windshield, cut-down doors (reprising the rakish look of the classic Darrin Packard), and a flush-fitting metal boot that completely concealed the Orlon acrylic fabric convertible top when it was lowered. While many of these same features would begin appearing on GM models throughout the 1950s, they were first seen on the Eldorado.

The car's interior was another Harley Earl and Bill Mitchell tour de force, featuring an embossed instrument panel stretching the entire width of the dashboard and wrapping into the door panels. The dashboard was accented with a leather-covered cowling sweeping around into the tops of the doors. Limited to only 532 cars, all of this exclusivity came at a hefty price of $7,750 (more than the average American earned in a year in 1953), making it the most expensive car in the Cadillac line.

Did You Know?

The Cadillac tailfin was inspired by the dramatically profiled twin-tail rudders of the World War II Lockheed P-38 fighter plane. In 1942 GM design chief Harley Earl sent a group of stylists to study the then top-secret aircraft, which was being tested at Selfridge Field near Detroit. After the war, Earl's protégé, Cadillac design chief Bill Mitchell, introduced the tailfin design on the 1948 models.

Continental was the name chosen by Edsel Ford for Lincoln's luxurious, custom-built coupes and cabriolets of the 1940s. Though the Continental was a success, World War II brought an abrupt end to its production in 1942. The cars were reprised from 1946 through 1948, and the name was resurrected again in 1956–1957 for the MK II and has remained a Lincoln trademark ever since—except for a brief period in 1955 when the Continental name was proudly worn on the fenders of a Porsche. It was a one-year-only (October 1954 through October 1955) moniker for the German sports cars. Once they began appearing on American roads, Ford Motor Company "suggested" that Porsche stop using the name.

1955 PORSCHE 356 CONTINENTAL

Price: $3,695 (approximately)

Engine: Four-cylinder, horizontally opposed

Displacement: 1,500cc (91.5 cubic inches)

Output: 70 horsepower

Gearbox: Four-speed synchromesh

Production: Approximately 200 with Continental badging

The cabriolet was Porsche's top-of-the-line model. It came equipped with a 1,500cc (91.5-cubic-inch) engine (also later a 1,600cc/97.5-cubic-inch engine), a fully upholstered and carpeted

interior, more comfortable seating compared to the standard model, a convertible top with a full, padded headliner, and amenities such as an interior dashboard light and an optional Telefunken (tube-type) radio with push-button tuning.

In 1954 American Porsche importer Max Hoffman told Porsche that Americans wanted cars with names not numbers, and he suggested the 1955 models should all have names. He had already established this precedent with Porsche's limited production America Roadster in 1952 and with the Speedster in 1954. At Hoffman's suggestion, the 1955 Porsche 356 coupes and cabriolets were named Continental, to reflect their European origins. By the time Ford Motor Company noted its objections, Stuttgart coachbuilder Karosserie Reutter had already punched holes in about 200 sets of front fenders and attached the stylish Continental signature script nameplates!

Under the louvered rear deck lid, the 356 models used a Porsche-built 1500cc flat, horizontally opposed four-cylinder engine developing 55 horsepower at 4,400 rpm. Fuel was fed by two Solex 32 PBI carburetors. The cars were also available with the more powerful 1500S engine, which delivered 70 horsepower at 5,000 rpm. The 1955 Continental Cabriolet pictured (1 of only 10 in the world known to have survived) marked the end of a brief era at Porsche.

Did You Know?

Hoffman Motors took delivery of its first three Porsches in 1950. Hoffman displayed one at the Concours d'Elegance at Watkins Glen, New York, where the Porsche won the trophy for "Most Interesting Car." With its rear-mounted, horizontally opposed, air-cooled four-cylinder engine and aerodynamic body styling, the 356 was nothing else if not interesting! In 1952 Hoffman would return to Watkins Glen behind the wheel of a new 356 Cabriolet and proudly drive off with the "Best Looking Car" award.

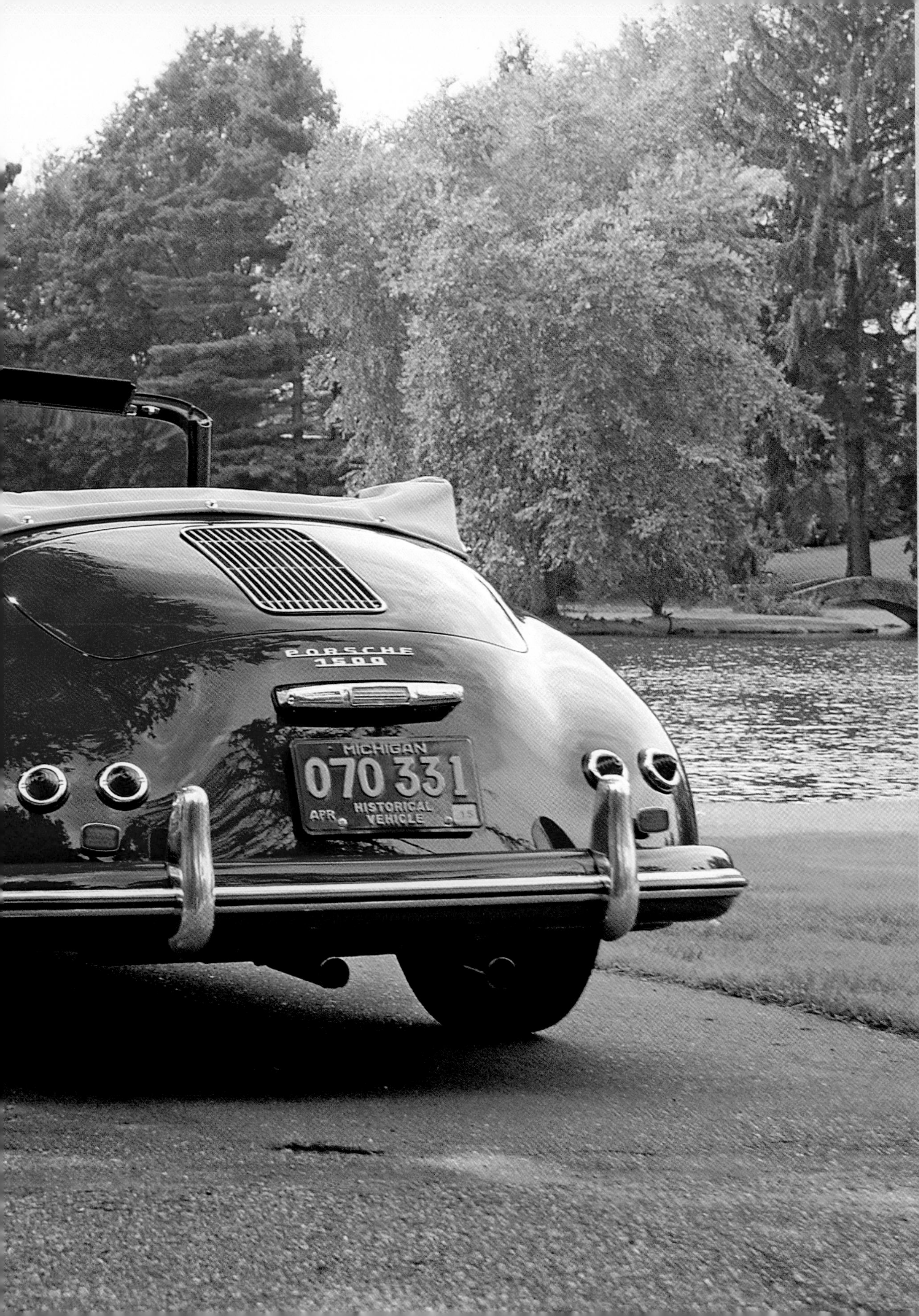

1955 PORSCHE 356 CONTINENTAL

The BMW 507 Sport Roadster is one of those rare cars that became a success after first being a failure, a failure that came at BMW's own hands. To compete with the much heralded new Mercedes-Benz 300SL, BMW developed the 507 Sport Roadster, which was already in prototype form for the 37th Frankfurt Motor Show in September 1955, a little over 18 months after the 300 SL's debut.

Built on a 97.6-inch (2.48-m) wheelbase, the 507 used a bizarre but highly effective combination of independent front and solid axle rear that endowed the car with excellent handling and cornering capabilities. Fitted with large 16-inch (41-cm)

1957 BMW 507

Price: $9,000
Engine: Aluminum alloy OHV V-8
Displacement: 3,168 cc (193.32 cubic inches)
Output: 150 horsepower
Gearbox: Floor-mounted four-speed manual
Production: 253

wheels, the 507 Sport Roadster had an impressively wide stance. The passenger compartment was lean, narrowed at the waist, and fitted with sporty cutaway doors.

Under the long stretch of hood was a revised V-8 that delivered an impressive 150 horsepower at 5,000 rpm. Using a conventional floor-mounted four-speed gearbox, the 507 was capable of 137 miles per hour (220.48 km/hr), making it one of the fastest cars on the market, second only to the 300 SL. Compared to the Mercedes, the BMW was a far more graceful-looking sports car and should have been a rousing success. New York importer Max Hoffman had envisioned selling several hundred 507 Sport Roadsters a year at a price of $5,000 each. However, production for 1956 was negligible, and the following year BMW built less than 100. Unlike Mercedes-Benz, which had an efficient assembly line, BMW was manufacturing the aluminum-bodied 507s almost by hand. Making matters worse, labor costs were soaring, and by the time the cars reached Hoffman's dealership, the retail price had increased to $9,000. Over a period of four years, BMW managed to build only 253 cars.

Did You Know?

The 507 body was almost entirely hand built from aluminum. BMW lost money on every 507 it sold, even with a final retail price in 1959 of $10,500. One of the first of many famous BMW 507 owners was Elvis Presley, who purchased his car in Germany while he was serving in the U.S. Army. When he brought it back to home, he had the engine swapped out for a Ford 289 V-8!

Convertibles were big business in the 1950s. After World War II, Americans wanted to get out and enjoy life after four years of gas rationing, lights out, and hard times. Nothing made that statement better than a new convertible. With Ford convertibles in three out of the top five sales positions by 1957, this was truly Dearborn's year to shine. However, despite record sales, the benchmark car for 1957 was not a Ford. It was the new Chevrolet Bel Air convertible.

After a stunning 1955 model launch with the Chevy V-8 engine, the company had restyled its cars for 1956 and again in 1957, saving the best for

1957 CHEVROLET BEL AIR

Price: $2,511 (base price)
Engine: Fuel-injected V-8
Displacement: 283 cubic inches (4.6 liters)
Output: 283 horsepower
Gearbox: Turboguide automatic
Production: Approximately 48,000 for 1957 model year

last. The 1957 Chevrolet Bel Air convertible was the GM division's styling and performance pièce de résistance. The final phase of Chevy's three-year plan culminated with fins and chrome, raising the

rear fenders to new heights and accentuating the revised 1957 grille work with Cadillac-inspired bumper guards and a bold Chevrolet bowtie emblem.

When the restyled 1957 models hit dealer showrooms, buyers were offered a choice of seven different V-8s, with outputs ranging from 162 horsepower all the way up to a whopping 283 horsepower. At the top of the option list was Chevy's brand-new 283-cubic-inch (4.6-l), 283-horsepower fuel-injected V-8 with a 10.5:1 compression ratio. It was the magic number, one horsepower per cubic inch. The 1957 Fuelie was

nothing short of a production line hot rod. Chevy advertising touted, "The Road Isn't Built That Can Make It Breathe Hard!" Coupled with a new, optional Turboglide automatic transmission, offering a built-in "kickdown" feature, the 1957 fuel-injected Bel Airs had almost unrivaled passing power. As history will attest, the 283 Chevy passed just about every car built in the 1950s, becoming not only the most popular model of its time but also one of the most prized collector cars ever built.

Did You Know?

The 1957 Bel Air had quite a lead-in the year before, when a 1956 Bel Air, driven by Zora Arkus-Duntov, shattered a 21-year record by making the 12.42-mile (19.9-km) ascent up Pikes Peak in 17 minutes, 24.05 seconds. The previous record was 19 minutes, 25.70 seconds. The road up Pikes Peak climbed through 170 sharp turns and cutbacks to the summit, 14,110 feet (4,302 m) above sea level. It was not only a good test of the car's suspension and handling but also proved the power and acceleration capabilities of the Chevy V-8.

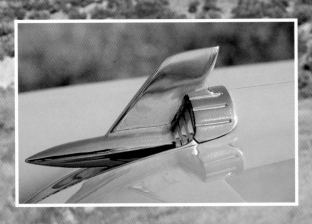

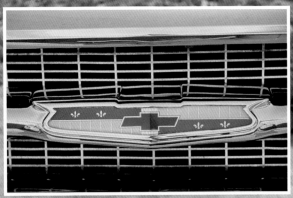

CHAPTER 7
HIGH-PERFORMANCE ERA—1960s AND 1970s MUSCLE CARS

Though some will disagree, the muscle car was really born in the 1950s with the original Chrysler 300. Chrysler's theory of packing a high-performance engine under the hood of what was otherwise a family car, like the 1955 Chrysler, and then sending it out to race in AAA and NASCAR competition was merely a means to an end. A racing victory, even then, was the best advertising an automaker could get. These otherwise nondescript-looking Chryslers began racking up a succession of victories in 1956, making the 300B the champion of American stock car racing. Chrysler's early success put the Letter Cars on the map, and by the early 1960s, every American automaker had a high-performance model.

In the late 1950s, GM's Bunkie Knudsen coined a marketing adage: "You can sell a young man's car to an old man, but you cannot sell an old man's car to a young man." Knudsen advocated design changes at GM that would lead to enterprising decisions in the early 1960s by innovative thinkers such as DeLorean and exciting new models such as the Pontiac GTO.

The success of the legendary Pontiac GTO encouraged Detroit to not only push the envelope but to reinvent it with cars like the groundbreaking 1964 1/2 Mustang, the 1970 Plymouth Hemi 'Cuda, and a wild array of midsize and full-size high-performance convertibles, from the Chrysler 300F in 1960 to the last of the great Hemi Mopar muscle cars in 1971. It was a brief but very memorable period that left us some of the most interesting cars of the past century.

The 1955 Chrysler 300 was the first of the famed Letter Cars, and the number *300* wasn't just a random choice by someone in marketing. The Chrysler delivered a wheel-spinning 300 horsepower when you dropped the hammer, and in 1955 that was really something. For the next decade, these special Chrysler models would be distinguished annually by a different letter in the 300 emblem.

Mechanix Illustrated's automotive editor, Tom McCahill, aptly described the first Chrysler 300s as "competition cars in a full Brooks Brothers suit," and he wasn't far from wrong. The 300s were doing great at Daytona and in motorsports competition, but aside from turning a fast quarter-mile, the

1960 CHRYSLER 300F

Price: $5,336

Engine: V-8 with Crossram induction manifold

Displacement: 413 cubic inches (6.76 liters)

Output: 400 horsepower

Gearbox: Four-speed manual synchromesh (optional)

Production: 1,212 (248 convertibles)

stodgy-looking Chryslers couldn't turn heads at a stoplight. Then something wonderful happened at Chrysler: Virgil Exner.

GM and Ford stylists were blown away when they saw Exner's 1957 models. The entire Chrysler

model line sprouted tail fins of exceptional proportions and sleek, sporty body lines. Exner had done away with Chrysler's old man's car image in one bold stroke. But he had saved the very best for the 300C, distinguished from all other 1957 models by a massive grille that virtually consumed the front end of the car.

For 1958 the letter was *D*, and the 300 came equipped with a 392 engine rated at 380 horsepower in standard trim and at 390 horses with optional Bendix electronic fuel injection. The 300E for 1959 upped the ante with a new 413-cubic-inch (6.76-liter) V-8 developing 380 horsepower but was a very limited edition, with only 140 convertibles

and 550 hardtop coupes built. Waiting in the wings for 1960 was Chrysler's ultimate letter car, the 300F.

The end result of Exner's ambition to create the fastest and best-styled automobile in America, the 300F became the greatest high-performance family car ever built. With an optional V-8 displacing 413 cubic inches (6.76 l) and equipped with a 30-inch (76.2-cm) Crossram induction manifold, the 300F delivered an unprecedented 400 horsepower, giving Chrysler unchallenged possession of the American road in 1960. The Chrysler 300F has become the number-one Letter Car of all time and one of the rarest, with only 248 convertibles and 964 coupes produced.

Did You Know?

The 300F offered a list of options almost as long as the car itself, which measured 18.3 feet (5.57 m) from the projecting Chrysler hood line to the tip of its canted tail fins. Among the most fascinating choices on the option list for 1960 were six-way power seats with dual swivel front buckets and, for truly sports-minded drivers, a limited slip rear differential and a four-speed manual synchromesh transmission. During 1960 Chrysler 300F models won the first six places in the flying mile at Daytona, with the winning car averaging 144 miles per hour (231 km/hr)!

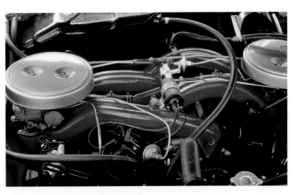

When the new 327 powerplant joined the Chevy lineup in 1962, it was a big performance step down from the formidable 409, but in truth, that was only a matter of degrees. After a full year in production, people were rallying around the 327. In full tune with dual quads, the 409 delivered 425 horsepower in 1963 (the rating in 1962 had been 409, but most say that was conservative), but it was a nasty, gas-gulping engine better suited to the drag strip than the street. In comparison, the 327 small-block in the SS put down 300 horsepower and just like the 340/409 could pull away like a rocket sled and lay enough rubber to make people wince for half a block.

1963 CHEVROLET IMPALA SS

Price: $3,185

Engine: L74 V-8

Displacement: 327 cubic inches (5.35 liters)

Output: 300 horsepower

Gearbox: Four-speed manual or Powerglide automatic

Production: 153,271 (SS-equipped models)

For 1963 the Impala received a minor facelift and was better looking than ever, with razor-edge lines along the entire length of the body, a sportier interior and instrument panel, and a new center

console with a shifter plate between the front seats for a four-speed manual or Powerglide automatic. Drivers were reminded of the car they were driving by a bold SS steering wheel emblem and swirl pattern insert on the instrument panel and center console. Although they looked larger and heavier, the 1963 Impala Super Sports were actually a bit lighter than their predecessors.

Having become something of an image car, the Impala SS was usually ordered with a full complement of luxury and comfort options: Powerglide, power steering and brakes, the latest version of All-Weather air conditioning, power windows, power seats, dual rear antennae (one was a dummy), AM/FM radio, and bumper guards.

The 1963 Super Sport option (RPO Z03) for the Impala Sport Coupe and Convertible featured circled SS rear fender emblems, body side moldings and rear cove panel with swirl-pattern silver inserts, and Super Sport wheel covers with stylized tri-bar spinners. On the interior, individual front bucket seats, all-vinyl upholstery, locking center consoles, shift plates (four-speed and Powerglide), and Super Sport emblems were standard.

Did You Know?

In 1963 Chevrolet sold 3 out of every 10 cars registered for the year in the United States, and total annual Chevrolet production exceeded 2.3 million cars. The 409 V-8 was an extra $428; the 300-horsepower 327 V-8 with four-barrel carburetors added $245. SS-equipped models reached a total of 153,271 cars, but Chevrolet never broke that number down into specific body styles. A total of 16,920 cars, most of which were Super Sports, were listed as equipped with the 409 V-8.

It was really a 1965 model, but Ford made a point of introducing the car on April 17, 1964, to totally catch the crosstown competition off guard and also to qualify as the Official Pace Car for the 1964 Indianapolis 500.

The first Mustangs were available in three body styles—hardtop coupe, convertible, and fastback. Ford's pony car theme extended from the grille emblem, a galloping Mustang, to the herd of horses running pell-mell across the deluxe seat back upholstery. The body styling was as trendsetting as the very notion of the car, introducing what would come to be known industrywide as the long-hood, short-rear-deck design, copied over the years by virtually every automaker in the world.

The car made such popular features as bucket seats and a center console-mounted shifter standard and offered a choice of three transmissions (two manual gearboxes and one automatic) and three engines: a 120-horsepower, six-cylinder; a 260-cubic-inch (4.26-l), 164-horsepower V-8 (replaced late in 1964 by a 200-horsepower 289); and a 289-cubic-inch (4.73-l), 210-horsepower V-8 (later replaced by a 225-horsepower four-barrel 289). Beginning in June 1964, a high-performance 289 option developing 271 horsepower was added as the

top-of-the-line model, giving buyers a full range of styles and performance options.

Some people wanted more than what Ford was offering, however, and their desires did not go long unrequited. By 1965 Carroll Shelby had started offering specially built and performance-tuned versions of the Mustang under the model designation GT 350. This was exactly the car aficionados had hoped the original Mustang would be. From a Shelby Mustang, however, more power and Cobra-like handling were expected. Shelby ordered cars with just about everything deleted, from the wheel covers and grille bars to the hood and springs. Shelby American rebuilt the engines and suspensions while also changing the hood, nose, and grille. All GT 350s came with a special instrument pod in the middle of the dashboard housing a tachometer and oil pressure gauge. The Shelby team modified the 289 V-8, boosting its output to 306 horsepower with an aluminum Cobra high-rise intake manifold and a 715-cfm Holley center-pivot float carburetor, finned aluminum Cobra valve covers, an extra-capacity aluminum oil pan, and Tri-Y exhaust headers.

1964 ½ FORD MUSTANG

Price: $2,795 (Shelby GT 350: $4,311)

Engine: 289 V-8

Displacement: 289 cubic inches (4.73 liters)

Output: 271 horsepower (Shelby GT 350: 306 horsepower)

Gearbox: Choice of three-speed, four-speed, or automatic transmission

Production: 121,538 (coupes and convertibles total, first model year)

Did You Know?

Mustang is the most recognized name in Ford Motor Company history. All of the 1965 GT 350s were fastback coupes. In 1966 Carroll Shelby built six special GT 350 convertibles, which he gave away to friends and employees! Beginning in 1967, Shelby models were offered in both coupe and convertible form.

In 1962, with Daytona and two SCCA class titles under its belt, the Corvette was in the second year of a two-year transition in body styling, which was to segue into the second-generation Corvette and the famed 1963 Sting Ray Coupe. When the Sting Ray was introduced, it was as if Chevrolet had reinvented the Corvette. Engines were completely revamped, from the cooling system to the Rochester fuel injection—the first major overhaul of the design since its introduction in 1957. The suspension was completely new, a fully independent layout that endowed the cars with unprecedented cornering ability and world-class road handling.

1967 CHEVROLET CORVETTE L71 ROADSTER

Price: $6,491 (approximately, equipped as pictured)

Engine: Chevrolet big-block V-8

Displacement: 427 cubic inches (7 liters)

Output: 435 horsepower

Gearbox: Four-speed manual (optional close ratio four-speed and close ratio heavy duty)

Production: 3,754 L71 optioned models

The Sting Ray's new V-8 delivered 360 horsepower posthaste, burying the tachometer

through every gear and launching the car from 0 to 60 in 5.6 seconds, through the quarter-mile in 14.2 seconds at 102 miles per hour (164 km/hr), and reaching a top speed of 151 miles per hour (243 km/hr). Wrote *Road & Track* after testing an early production model with the 360 engine and 3.70:1 final drive, "As a purely sporting car, the new Corvette will know few peers on road or track."

The most exciting Corvette of the 1960s (for the street) was the 1967 L71 option, a 427 developing an honest 435 horsepower with an 11:1 compression ratio, solid lifters, and transistorized electronic ignition. Topped by a triangular air cleaner covering a new manifold fitted with three Holley two-barrel carburetors, the L71 offered unrivaled performance.

The body design was the Corvette's most aggressive look ever, with a huge hood bulge and bold, vented, outside exhaust pipes running from wheel opening to wheel opening. A tribute of sorts to form over function, a good part of the L71's performance impression was made without even starting the engine. Just looking at the car was enough to cause an adrenalin rush. The most powerful street cars of their time, L71 Corvettes left an indelible impression on the American motoring scene.

Did You Know?

The side-mount exhaust system was one of the Corvette styling department's most inspired projects. The amount of work that went into its design was astounding, especially when you consider that it was painstakingly done by the most notorious high-volume division of GM. The complex exhaust system, inspired by the 427 Cobra, was designed so that the outside surface of the side exhausts should "not exceed the temperature that the skin of the car would reach in the sun of Arizona." This was achieved by designing a double-layer protective shroud around the exhaust pipe, ventilated for cooling on the outside and polished on the inside of the inner layer to reflect heat back to the pipe. No one got burned, especially with an option price of only $134.50!

In 1966, when the next-generation Barracuda was being sketched out, the Ford Mustang had already established the pony car concept. Chrysler also knew that Chevrolet was at work on a model to compete with Mustang (which turned out to be the Camaro). Whatever the Dodge and Plymouth designers did, the niche had already been established. What they needed to do was redefine it.

Looking at the 'Cuda's competition in 1970, the Mustang's styling was pretty aggressive, while the Camaro's was a bit softer. The Plymouth design team had taken a gamble with

1971 PLYMOUTH HEMI 'CUDA

Price: $4,283 (approximately)
Engine: Hemi V-8
Displacement: 426 cubic inches (6.98 liters)
Output: 425 horsepower
Gearbox: Four-speed manual
Production: Seven (convertibles)

the Barracuda, with its radical departure from contemporary Chrysler styling. Fortunately, Plymouth had a very active, hands-on vice president of design by the name of Elwood Engle,

and he had some definite thoughts on the car and what it should be. The 1970 Plymouth 'Cuda simply blew everyone in Detroit away. It made the Mustang look old, the Camaro and Firebird tame, the GTO heavy-handed, and all the rest—the 4-4-2, the Chevelle, and so on—just big cars with big engines. In one bold stroke, Plymouth had redefined the high-performance market for the coming decade.

Giving each of the Barracuda models something of a unique identity was part of the design program. The top of the line Hemi 'Cuda was distinguished by the shaker air scoop protruding through the hood, but the design was not intended solely for that model. It was also available as an option on the 440 six pack and on down to the 383 and 340 as well. Other details, such as like hood pins, decals, and fog lamps, were used to distinguish different Barracuda models.

For Plymouth 1970 and 1971 were pretty good years; for muscle car and pony car enthusiasts they were great years. Unfortunately, the muscle car era soon came to an abrupt end at the hands of the federal government, OPEC, and the nation's insurance companies. The last great Hemi 'Cuda convertible would be built in 1971.

Did You Know?

In 1971 dealers could barely give Hemi cars away. Plymouth built only seven 1971 Hemi 'Cuda convertibles, and only two of those were equipped with a four-speed manual transmission. You are looking at pictures of one-half of the entire 1971 production of four-speed Hemi 'Cuda convertibles! All 'Cuda models were specially built with suspensions designed for the output of the car. The high-performance 440 and Hemi models were equipped with extra-heavy-duty torsion bars and stabilizer bars, heavy-duty shock absorbers, special rear suspensions, and Dana 60 rear ends with 9-3/4-inch (24.7-cm) ring gears.

CHAPTER 8
EUROPEAN CONVERTIBLES: TOPS DOWN AND REVS UP!

Convertibles are timeless symbols of youth, freedom, and vitality embodied by three essential ingredients: visual appeal, engineering, and performance. When an automaker gets that recipe just right, the result is an object that preys upon our emotions, lingers in our thoughts, and leaves us consumed by an unrest that is only quelled by slipping behind the wheel. Nowhere else in the world is this better known than in England, Germany, and Italy, where convertibles come in all sizes and all prices, and the term "age appropriate" has no meaning.

For decades, the lower end of the European convertible market was occupied by two very historic initials: "MG." For those of modest means, MG was the answer. The question really wasn't important. If it involved sports car club racing in the postwar 1950s, the answer was almost always MG.

By the early 1950s, British automakers Jaguar, MG, and Austin-Healey had become established brands in America. Meanwhile, German automakers Porsche, Mercedes-Benz, and BMW were also beginning to get a foothold on U.S. shores, as was Enzo Ferrari's first line of road cars, mostly through importers such as Max Hoffman in New York and John von Neumann in Los Angeles.

Of the British marques, Austin-Healey and MG were the most affordable and, for sports car club racers, the easiest to set up for competition on the weekend and to drive on the street the rest of the week. But the two cars had a lot more in common than practicality. The Austin Motor Company had merged with MG in 1952 to form the BMC conglomerate, and that same year the Austin-Healey 100 was introduced at the London Motor Show. Graceful but sturdy and competitively priced, the 100 became an instant sensation. The visual relationship between the Austin-Healey 100 and the 1955 MGA is unmistakable, as MG greatly benefited from the merger with Austin. The more sporting of the two marques, the Austin-Healey models 100, 100M, and 100-6 were popular on both road and track. The 100-6 was the first of the "big Healeys" to offer a six-cylinder engine and even greater performance. The 2,639-cc (161-cubic-inch) engine delivered 102 horsepower at 4,600 rpm and a top speed of 103 miles per hour (166 km/hr), making it the fastest Healey up to that time. The model pictured is a 1958 100-6.

Between 1950 and 1960, advances in design, engineering, and—most importantly—marketing had driven up interest in Porsche, Ferrari, Mercedes-Benz, and Jaguar to record levels. BMW was having a bit more difficult time of it back then. The greatest early successes for European automakers really came in the 1960s, when established dealers all across America were selling the leading European marques almost as easily Fords, Chevys, and Cadillacs.

"Niche marketing" was not yet a term, but it was very much a practice of necessity for automakers such as Porsche and Ferrari, who had only sports cars to sell, while the lion's share of import business was going to the very top and bottom ends of the market through Mercedes-Benz and Volkswagen. By the time of the first OPEC oil crisis in the 1970s, European cars were an established part of the American landscape, and while Detroit struggled with downsizing, economizing, and fuel and safety standards, the European imports, convertibles in particular, were still thriving within their own segment of the market. It is from 1960 to the early 1990s that we find some of the most attractive and desirable European convertibles.

For nearly a decade, the MG was the most commonly raced sports car in America. Throughout the early 1950s, MG TC and TD models were very competitive cars, especially when fitted with special oversize valves, milled heads, domed pistons, and higher compression ratios to extract every trace of horsepower possible from their small four-cylinder engines. The cars were nevertheless dated and outclassed, if not in engineering and suspension then certainly in appearance. That was all about to change in 1955. From the time of its debut at the Frankfurt Auto Show, on September 22, 1955, the MGA was lauded as an instant success by the world's motoring press. *Road*

1960 MGA TWIN CAM

Price: $3,345
Engine: Four-cylinder
Displacement: 1,588 cc (96.6 cubic inches)
Output: 108 horsepower
Gearbox: Four-speed manual
Production: 2,111

& Track wrote, "Early enthusiasm for its appearance can now be augmented by the knowledge of its very surprising performance. Anybody who likes anything about sports cars will be more than pleased with the

new MG." Automotive enthusiasts wholeheartedly agreed, making the MGA the most popular sports car ever built by the time it went out of production in June 1962. Over seven years, MG sold more than 100,000 MGAs, including a limited production run of 2,111 Twin Cam roadsters and coupes, manufactured from September 1958 through June 1960.

The MGAs had a pleasant, raspy tone to their exhaust note, a firm ride, agile handling, and, for the engine displacement and size, spirited performance. Though the MGA's 1500 B series engine shared most of its parts with BMC's other products, it was modified to increase performance, developing an ample 72 horsepower at 5,750 rpm, 108 horsepower in the Twin Cam. Owners had a choice of two gearboxes: the standard four-speed or a close-ratio gear set based on the MGA competition cars campaigned at Le Mans in 1955. The suspension utilized an independent front with coil springs and unequal-length wishbones; the rear was a semi-elliptic leaf-spring arrangement. If nothing else, the Le Mans cars had proven the durability of the MGA's underpinnings, utilizing essentially the same components for competition as the production cars.

Did You Know?

The aerodynamic efficiency of the MGA body design quickly proved its worth, returning an average increase in top speed of 15 miles per hour (24 km/hr) over its predecessors with no increase in horsepower. MGAs were so trim that they could maintain a speed of 60 miles per hour (97 km/hr) on only 16 horsepower. As a J production racer, the MGA Twin Cam was successful, bringing countless victories to MG in the hands of privateer drivers the world over. But for daily driving, it was far more difficult to manage than the MGA 1500 and later Mk II 1600s. The standard MGA would ultimately prove to be the better of the two.

In the 1960s, Ferrari burst upon the American motoring scene with one spectacular road car after another. But the one that would leave the most lasting impression was a convertible built almost exclusively for the U.S. market at the request of Ferrari importers Luigi Chinetti Sr. and John von Neumann.

"In Italy, it was hard for the factory to understand a convertible as a serious fast car," Luigi Chinetti Jr. told the author. "To them, high speed was the domain of the closed car, the Berlinetta, which in Italian means 'little sedan,' a lightweight, streamlined body trimmed for racing." However, in New York Chinetti Sr.'s customers were clamoring for an aggressively styled convertible. The same was true on the West

1961 FERRARI 250GT SPYDER CALIFORNIA

Price: $11,600
Engine: 60-degree V-12
Displacement: 2,953 cc (180 cubic inches)
Output: 280 horsepower
Gearbox: Four-speed syncromesh
Production: Approximately 105 SHB adn LHB models

Coast, where sports car distributor and race driver John Von Neumann was telling Enzo Ferrari that the standard 250GT Cabriolet was not the kind of car his customers wanted. "It was with great reluctance

that Mr. Ferrari acquiesced to building these cars for the American market," said Chinetti Jr. "Ironically, the 250GT Spyder California turned out to be the most successful Ferrari model sold in this country up to that time!"

The now-coveted 250GT SWB (short-wheelbase) Spyder California made its debut at the Geneva Salon in March 1960. The cars were produced in two series: the long wheelbase, of which fewer than 50 were built, and the short wheelbase, a lighter-weight, steel-and-aluminum-bodied version, introduced in 1960 and built through 1963. The total was again around 50 examples.

The LWB Spyder California was produced in three series. About seven cars were built before the new LWB 250GT Berlinetta engine and chassis were utilized. It is estimated that 27 second-series cars were produced between the end of 1958 and the end of 1959.

The Spyder California, in either wheelbase, was one of the first Ferraris to be described as a "driver's car"—a car that was capable of exceptional speed and handling yet comfortable and luxurious enough for daily driving. The last example (4167 GT) was sold in the United States in February 1963.

Did You Know?

Enzo Ferrari did not want to build the 250GT Spyder California because the company already had a 250GT Cabriolet. However, while that car was popular in Europe, American buyers wanted the same performance and aggressive styling that was offered with the 250GT Berlinetta and 250GT SWB, which became the eventual platform for the Spyder California. Had Ferrari not built the cars for Chinetti and von Neumann, it is very likely they would have taken SWB Berlinettas and had Scaglietti convert them into Spyders. How do we know? Because when Enzo Ferrari refused to make a 275 GTB/4 Spyder in 1967, that's exactly what Chinetti did to 10 GTB/4 Berlinettas!

In the mid-1950s, Luigi Chinetti Sr. moved his Ferrari dealership from New York to Greenwich, Connecticut, and formed the North American Racing Team (NART) to campaign Ferraris in the United States. The factory even gave Chinetti the right to use the *Cavallino Rampante* ("Prancing Horse") emblem as part of the NART insignia. But in 1966 there arose a difference of opinion between Chinetti Sr. and Enzo Ferrari—one that was never resolved and that created a rift that the two men took to their graves.

In 1966 Ferrari refused Chinetti's request for a suitable car to replace the 250GT SWB Spyder

1967 FERRARI 275 GTS/4 NART SPYDER

Price: $15,000
Engine: Double overhead cam 60-degree V-12
Displacement: 3,286 cc (200 cubic inches)
Output: 330 horsepower
Gearbox: Five-speed manual
Production: 10

California, insisting that Chinetti no longer needed to have special cars for his American clientele. Contrarily, Chinetti and his son decided to go out

on their own and have the cars they wanted built in Italy at their own expense in defiance of Ferrari. They commissioned Carrozzeria Scaglietti to take Ferrari's new 275 GTB/4 Berlinetta and convert it into a Spyder. Sergio Scaglietti was an artist when it came to fabricating custom coachwork, and the 10 Berlinetta bodies that Chinetti had redone into Spyders were flawless. The cars were all sold exclusively through Chinetti Motors in Greenwich as the 275 GTS/4 NART Spyder. Though few in number, and much to Enzo Ferrari's chagrin, the NART Spyder became one of the most coveted Ferrari models of all time.

The fenderlines of the 275 GTB/4 body lent themselves beautifully to the look of an open car. Using the same driveline as the 275 GTB/4 Berlinetta, which many consider the most beautiful Ferrari road car ever built, the NART Spyders were powered by a Colombo-based four-cam V-12, breathing through six Weber 40 DCN 17 carburetors and delivering up to 330 horsepower at 8,000 rpm through a five-speed manual gearbox. The Spyders were built atop a revised Tipo 596 all-independently suspended chassis, with the engine, prop-shaft tube, and transaxle all rigidly mounted along the frame, as on the new Ferrari 330 GTC.

Did You Know?

The car pictured here is the first NART Spyder. It was raced in 1967 at the 12 Hours of Sebring by two female drivers, Denise McCluggage and Pinkie Rollo. The car was painted a unique shade of "sun yellow"—*giallo solare*—which contrasted with its black leather interior. The NART Spyder was one of six Ferraris competing, and as the race progressed, the other five dropped out, leaving the pale yellow NART Spyder the sole Ferrari remaining. Any chance of a class victory faded during an ill-fated pit stop, when only three new tires could be found, forcing McCluggage back into the race with one worn tire. The additional time required to pit again and replace the fourth tire cost McCluggage and Rollo a class victory.

Until fall 1969, the only Mercedes-Benz V-8 available was the massive 6.3-liter (384-cubic-inch) used in the 600 series limousines and luxurious 300 SEL 6.3 sedans. Historically, Mercedes had relied on finely tuned four- and six-cylinder engines for its passenger car lines, and although smaller than the V-8s in many American automobiles, Daimler-Benz sixes produced nearly the same power by revving much higher, something that would benefit the company well in the troubled years of the 1970s.

Using the same performance theory applied to the inline six, engine rpm became relatively economical to obtain, and effective if the mixture

1971 MERCEDES-BENZ 280 SE 3.5 CABRIOLET

Price: $14,155

Engine: Single overhead cam fuel-injected V-8

Displacement: 3,499 cc (213 cubic inches)

Output: 230 horsepower

Gearbox: Four-speed automatic

Production: 1,232

was properly controlled by fuel injection. The 3.5-liter (213-cubic-inch) V-8 introduced with the 280 SE 3.5 was a marvel of engineering. It utilized a cast-iron block crowned by aluminum heads and

an extremely over-square combination of 92-mm stroke x 65.8-mm bore to achieve a swept volume of 3,499 cc. With the air–fuel mixture compressed at a ratio of 9.5:1, the fuel-injected SOHC V-8 developed an impressive 230 horsepower at 5,800 rpm. This was a magic equation in America—more than one horsepower per cubic inch!

The compact size and light weight of the new engine allowed it to fit the mature 280 SE chassis and provided it with youthful vitality. Despite the convertible's 110-inch (2.8-m) wheelbase, overall length of 196.2 inches (4.98 m), and weight of 3,640 pounds (1,651 kg), a 3.5 could arrive at 60 miles per hour (96 km/hr) from a standstill in 9.3 seconds and reach 130 miles per hour (209 km/hr). These were impressive numbers for a full-size luxury convertible.

The 280 SE 3.5 rode atop a fully independent coil-spring suspension with four-wheel disc brakes and an optional limited-slip differential. Overbuilt in typical Mercedes-Benz fashion, the convertible avoided the torsional flexing most open cars suffered by using a strengthened chassis with additional steel crossbraces below the leading edge of the rear seat and extending rearward under the trunk. On rough roads, body shudder and cowl shimmy were virtually nonexistent. Of all Mercedes-Benz models, this was perhaps the quintessential German-engineered luxury touring car.

Did You Know?

The convertible top on the Mercedes-Benz 280 SE 3.5 folded effortlessly into six layers of cloth, insulation, and padding. When closed, the convertible top was nearly 1.5 inches (3.8 cm) thick, providing superior insulation and soundproofing. With a top mechanism concealed from view by a fully padded interior headliner, the manufacturing of each 280 SE 3.5 Cabriolet top required more than 16 hours of hand assembly! Since only 13 cars per week could be built, the Cabriolet immediately became exclusive. Between 1970 and 1971, Daimler-Benz was able to deliver only 1,232 examples.

1971 MERCEDES-BENZ 280 SE 3.5 CABRIOLET

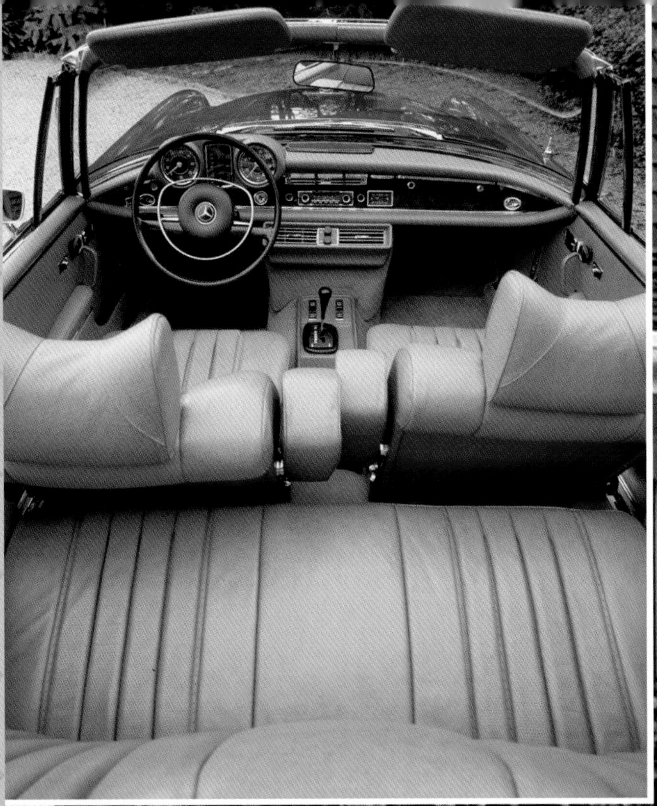

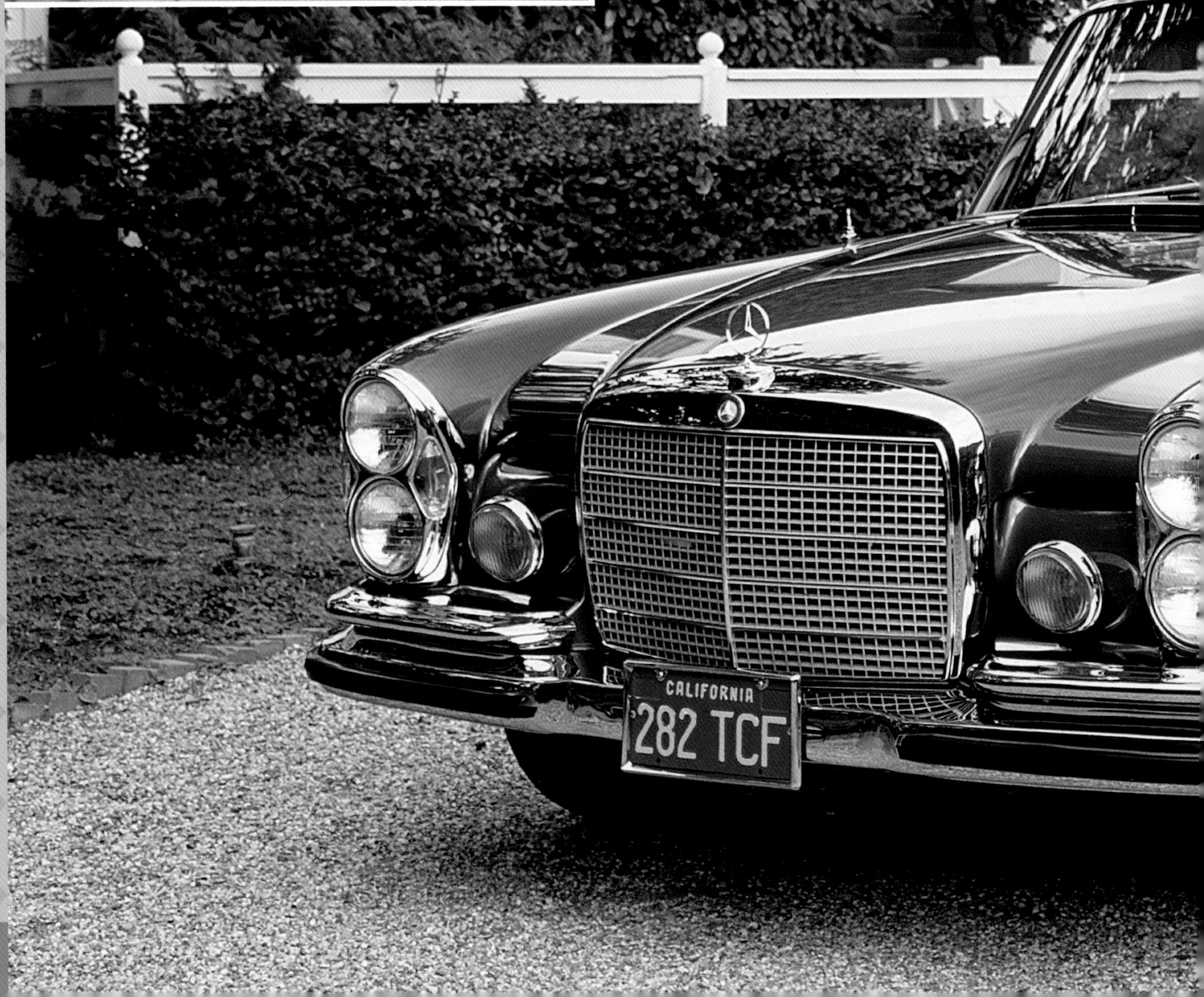

In the 1990s, almost every European automaker exporting cars to the United States offered a convertible. Jaguar, which always had a drophead in the model line, was scoring sales with one of the most striking two-door 2+2 sports models on the road, the XJS. In 1992 the XJS line was revised with a freshened taillight array, flared rocker panels, and new grille. Inside, the car was fitted with specially contoured sports seats and an all-new walnut-trimmed instrument cluster. From a purely aesthetic point of view, the XJS was without equal in terms of sheer, unadulterated luxury. Compared to the cold Teutonic environs of German cars in the early 1990s or the slathered-in-leather approach of Italian

1993 JAGUAR XJS CABRIOLET

Price: $56,750

Engine: Double overhead cam, four valves per cylinder, aluminum alloy straight six

Displacement: 4.0 liters (244 cubic inches)

Output: 223 horsepower

Gearbox: ZF four-speed dual-mode electronic automatic or Getrag five-speed manual

Production: 115,413

makes, the Jaguar blend of supple Connolly hides and polished walnut veneers was incomparable. The same could be said of the XJS convertible's headliner:

an exercise in preserving the dignity of a coupe when raised, deeply padded to filter out noise, and perfectly trimmed to conceal any trace of the elaborate folding mechanism within.

Of course, one had to dole out $56,750 for an XJS in 1993, and that was a lot of Franklins. For the money, the XJS delivered an equal measure of performance to luxury. Under the hood was a 223-horsepower, 4.0-liter (244-cubic-inch) six-cylinder engine, making the 1993 model the first six-cylinder convertible Jaguar had built since 1971!

Taking power to the ground was a limited slip rear and ZF four-speed dual-mode electronic automatic transmission. A five-speed manual gearbox by Getrag was available as an option. The XJS could manage 0 to 60 in 8.6 seconds and could reach a top speed of 138 miles per hour (222 km/hr).

Did You Know?

Originally the XJS was going to be called the XK-F, as it was initially regarded as a replacement for the venerable XK-E. The new car, however, had an entirely different character, and Jaguar decided to let the memory of the E-Type rest in peace. A stunning grand touring sports car, the XJS held its own for more than two decades of production. The last XJS was produced in April 1996, ending a 21-year production run. A 6-liter (366-cubic-inch), 12-cylinder engine was also available in the exclusive XJR-S coupe and convertible, but this version was limited to only 100 specially numbered vehicles.

1993 JAGUAR XJS CABRIOLET

1993 JAGUAR XJS CABRIOLET

Closing out the 1990s with a BMW can mean only one car, the Z3. This was the answer to the late twentieth century's "convertible to beat," the Porsche Boxster, and BMW gave its longtime rival a good run for the money as the millennium came to a close. There was a certain 1950s-era gentility to the Z3 2.8, a sensation of free-spirited driving that recalls old MGs, Healeys, and Porsche Speedsters, cars with lightweight fabric tops that could be unlatched with one hand and flung effortlessly over your head into a rippled pile. The 1998 BMW Z3 2.8 had that same carefree spirit and for around $40,000 was more sports car than anyone had a reasonable right to expect.

1998 BMW Z3

Price: $40,000

Engine: Aluminum-block double overhead cam inline six

Displacement: 2.8 liters (171 cubic inches)

Output: 189 horsepower

Gearbox: Getrag five-speed manual

Production: 297,087 produced from 1996 to 2002

At first glance, the Z3 body was odd looking: long in front and incredibly short in the rear. Overall, the Z3 was 16 inches (40.6 cm) shorter than a 3 Series, a fraction narrower, and 2.4

inches (6 cm) lower at the roofline than a BMW convertible. With a flash of historical lineage in the fender gills and BMW roundel, the Z3 was one car you either loved or hated; there was no middle ground. Since the current Z4 is an even wilder version of the Z3, the love overcame the hate.

The interior was cramped but comfortable, with exceptionally supportive high-back seats, logically positioned controls, and the quality of fit and finish BMW owners had come to expect in every model, price notwithstanding. At the heart of the Z3 was an aluminum-block DOHC 2.8-liter (171-cubic-inch)

inline six-cylinder engine. A straight six in a sports car was almost an anomaly by 1998, but BMW chose this well-seasoned configuration to position the engine's center of gravity farther back, giving the Z3 2.8 an almost ideal front/rear weight distribution. The 2.8 six filled the engine bay impressively, with sculptured styling that made looking at it almost as enjoyable as listening to it unwind on an open stretch of highway. The 189-horsepower six, coupled to a Getrag five-speed, made 0 to 60 pass by in 6.3 seconds.

Did You Know?

The Z3 was a modern-day version of the famous prewar-era BMW 328. By 1939 BMW 328s had scored more than 100 victories in competition and had become the world's fastest standard-production sports cars, capable of 0 to 60 in 10 seconds and a top speed of 95 miles per hour (153 km/hr). Sixty years later, the Z3 filled those shoes quite nicely, becoming the most successful model in the company's history.

CHAPTER 9
THE 21ST-CENTURY CONVERTIBLE

There are only a handful of constants in the universe. One of them is convertibles. Even when the light was about to go out for open cars in America during the late 1970s, when it was believed that the 1976 Cadillac Eldorado would be the "last American convertible," the desire for that swirling current of air rushing over the windshield never diminished. Until American convertibles made their return in the 1980s, European and Japanese cars kept the spirit alive on American roads, as did the torrent of restored older convertibles, which increased in value exponentially as every year went by. The 1970s left an indelible mark on American drivers, and it is no surprise that several of the most popular twenty-first-century convertibles—including the latest Ford Mustang GT and Shelby GT 500, which embody everything that makes 1970s Mustangs and Shelbys some of today's most valuable collector cars—take their styling cues from the glorious days of the American muscle car. After several years away, the Chevrolet Camaro returned in 2009, and has been such a big hit that GM launched production of a convertible model in late 2010. Yes, the Firebird is gone, as is Pontiac, but there is no shortage of American branded convertibles today.

The twenty-first century is very much like the 1950s, as every automaker the world over is striving to offer a car that has special appeal. While today's buyers are different and the marketplace has certainly changed, the fundamental desire for a convertible is as basic in 2011 as it was in 1911. Here, then, are five cars with heritage that keep us grounded in the realization that indeed, as the French say, *Plus ça change, plus c'est la même chose.*

"The more things change, the more they stay the same."

Since April 1964, the Mustang has been the most famous American 2+2 ever built. The Mustang literally established the market niche that is occupied today by dozens of sporty convertibles and coupes, cars defined by a style—long hood, short rear deck—that has been mimicked by every American, European, and other automaker for nearly half a century. The Mustang was the original, and in the twenty-first century, as in the twentieth, there is little that can rival Ford's legendary pony car.

In 2010 Ford gave its muscular, 1970s-influenced models a new exterior design that further accentuates the retro look of celebrated Mustang models such

2010 FORD MUSTANG GT

Price: $35,995

Engine: 90-degree V-8

Displacement: 281 cubic inches (4.6 liters)

Output: 315 horsepower

Gearbox: Five-speed automatic

Production: Still in production

as the Boss 302 and Mach 1. The company literally trumped its own high-performance retro look, introduced in 2005, with more aggressively sculpted front and rear fender wheel flares and a classic spear

character line on the doors that leads to a modern take on the 1970s "hip" rear fenders. The rear end design features aggressively angled rear corners and a more sculptured deck lid, but the overall look is like taking the old Boss 302 and slipstreaming the body contours.

Inside, the twenty-first century also handsomely collides with the 1970s by combining classic Mustang interior styling with world-class technology, creating a familiar look but incorporating the latest in instrumentation and safety features. These blend seamlessly into a car that feels like a well-worn driving glove when you slip behind the wheel.

The real retro touch, however, is what's under the hood: the same rousing V-8 performance of the muscle car era tamed by fuel-efficient technology and coupled to a state-of-the-art five-speed automatic (or manual) transmission, and suspension innovations in the limited-edition Bullitt model, including a 315-horsepower V-8.

Photos courtesy Ford Motor Company

Did You Know?

Ford sold more than 100,000 Mustangs between April and August 1964, achieving the most successful new vehicle launch in history. Over at General Motors, the Mustang's six-figure sales tally raised some executive eyebrows and caused GM management to green light the Camaro as a competitive model. Up until August 1964, GM hadn't been that impressed with Lee Iacocca's little 2+2 coupes and convertibles and had in fact considered the Chevrolet Corvair the Mustang's equal. The mind reels at such revelations!

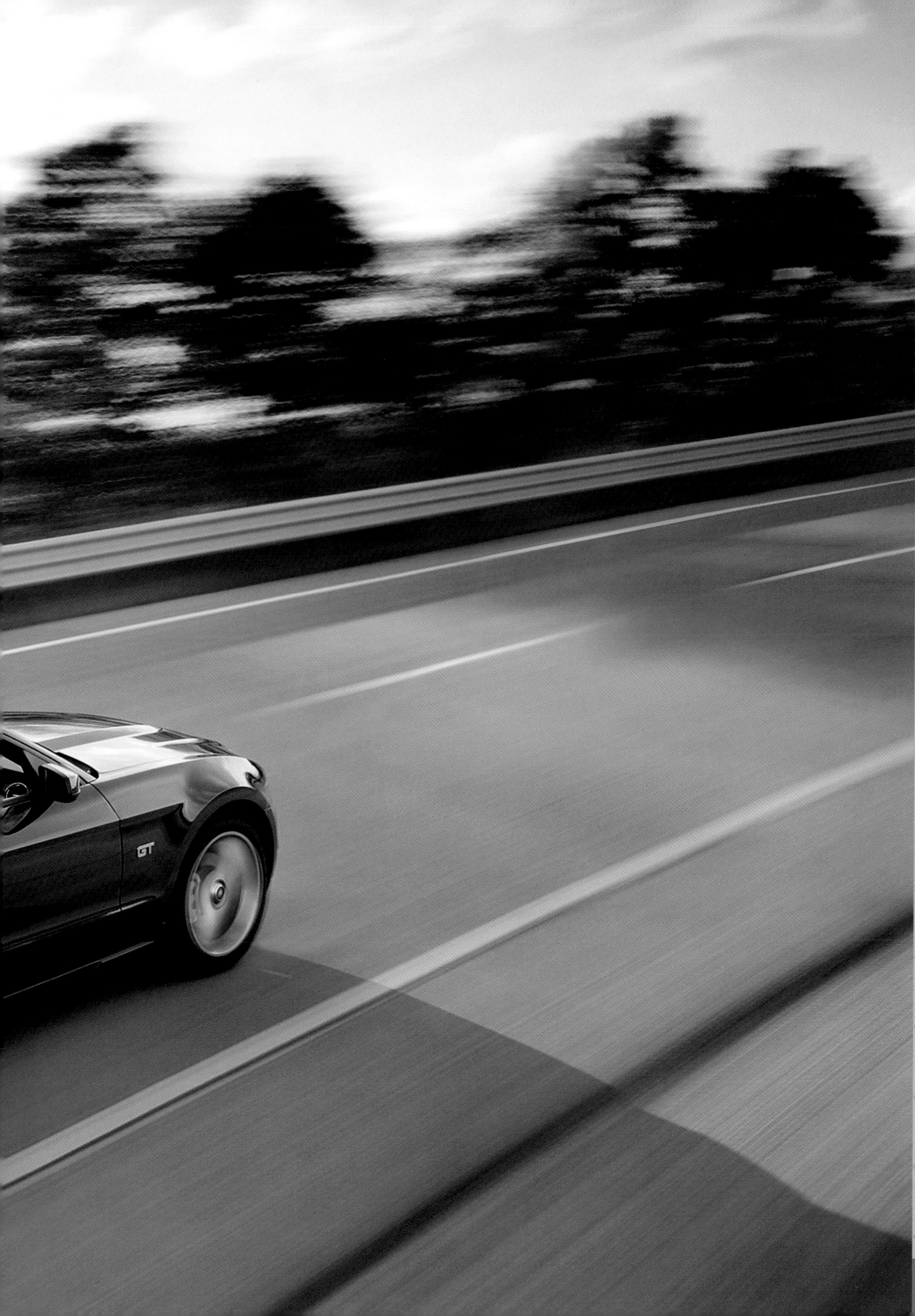

2010 FORD MUSTANG GT

In 1997 Mercedes-Benz achieved something it hadn't been able to do since the early 1960s. It created a model line that included not one, but two sports cars. More than 35 years had passed since Mercedes-Benz had offered the legendary 300 SL and 190 SL roadsters. When the 190 SL retired from the road in 1963, so too did the concept of a small, sporty two-seater from Germany's most legendary automaker. Enter the 1997 SLK. Powered by a DOHC, four-valve-per-cylinder engine, paired with a Roots-type supercharger, the SLK was the first supercharged Mercedes-Benz production car since 1939! It was also the first lower-priced SL since 1963 and

2010 MERCEDES-BENZ SLK

Price: $47,775 (SLK300); $50,175 (SLK350)

Engine: Supercharged twin-cam V-6

Displacement: 3.0/3.5 liters

Output: 228/300 horsepower

Gearbox: Seven-speed driver-adaptive automatic transmission with overdrive, touch shift, optimum gear programming, and comfort mode

Production: Still in production

the first-ever Mercedes-Benz with a retractable hardtop. At the touch of a button, the trunk opened in reverse and the hardtop folded and

stowed away. If you ran a stopwatch, it took only 22 seconds. You could do it at a stoplight without holding up traffic.

The latest SLK line features one of the most distinctive front end designs in the world, a look that is unmistakably Mercedes with a strong influence from the world of Formula 1 racing. The SLK's sleek nacelle nose is punctuated by the Mercedes star emblem, while at the rear, an apron incorporating an air diffuser and trapezoidal exhaust outlets equally define the back of the SLK. Inside, the SLK has chronometer-type gauges with aluminum accents, a three-spoke sport steering wheel, and an audio system with

an in-dash six-disk CD/DVD changer, as well as a Bluetooth interface that allows a cellular phone still in a pocket or purse to be operated through the car's audio system.

Surrounding a state-of-the-art, fully independent suspension and anti-lock braking and anti-skid control systems, the SLK's unibody uses an impressive amount of high-strength steel alloy—42 percent of the total structure—and the entire body shell is zinc-coated for long-term corrosion protection. The SLK also makes use of a scratch-resistant clear-coat paint developed in the nanotechnology sector. There are two standard models: the SLK 300 and the SLK 350, plus the high-performance AMG version.

Both the first and second series (twenty-first-century model) SLKs are true sports cars, cut from the same legendary cloth as the 190 SL, the MGA, the Jaguar XK-120, and the Porsche 356. The small, sporty two-seaters remind you what driving a sports car is all about. *Photos courtesy Mercedes-Benz USA*

2010 MERCEDES-BENZ SLK

Did You Know?

Mercedes-Benz pioneered supercharging. In 1921 Mercedes (still independent of Benz) introduced the 10/40/65 model, equipped with a supercharged four-cylinder, single-overhead cam engine. This was the first production motorcar in the world offered with a supercharger as standard equipment. Mercedes-Benz was also the first automaker in the 1950s with a fuel-injected production car engine. Both of these features are used on the SLK, which in 1997 was the first supercharged, four-cylinder, two-seat sports car that Mercedes-Benz had offered since 1939!

At the time of the demise of the last two front-engine Porsche sports cars, the 928 and the 968, Porsche had seen its sales and profits dramatically decline. To regain its profitability, the legendary German automaker chose to return to its roots as a niche sports car maker. To do so, it had to eliminate the costly manufacturing process of building three completely different models with virtually no shared parts and create two models with many shared parts. Thus the 911 series was retained and is the evergreen car that now defines Porsche. For an entry-level vehicle, it was equally

2010 PORSCHE BOXSTER

Price: $47,600 ($58,000 Boxster S)

Engine: Mid-mounted, water-cooled six-cylinder boxer

Displacement: 2.9 liters (177 cubic inches)

Output: 255 horsepower

Gearbox: PDK double-clutch

Production: Still in production

important to design a car that shared many of the 911's components, as well as familiar design cues. The answer was the Boxster, a combination of the

horizontally opposed Porsche "boxer" engine and the historic "speedster" design—Boxster. First produced in 1996, the new car was and remains a perfect blend of retro styling, strongly suggestive of the 1950s, combined with state-of-the-art Porsche suspension and transmission technology.

For the latest version of the Boxster, Porsche upgraded to a 2.9-liter (177-cubic-inch) "basic" powerplant that develops 255 horsepower and, in the high-performance Boxster S, a 3.4-liter (207-cubic-inch) engine that delivers 310 horsepower thanks to Direct Fuel Injection.

On the pavement, the Boxster gives up nothing in performance and handling to similarly priced competitors. With a surprisingly long body measuring 14.25 feet (4.3 m), set on a 95.2-inch (2.4-m) wheelbase, the Boxster's lengthy silhouette and ground-hugging center of gravity make it a virtual point-and-shoot car. Top track-tested speed, according to Porsche AG, is 157 miles per hour (253 km/hr), fast enough to bring back vivid images of Richard von Frankenberg at the Avus yet modern enough to return a 26.3 miles-per-gallon average. *Photos courtesy Porsche Cars North America*

Did You Know?

Fuel economy and performance, once two diametrically opposed objectives, now work hand in hand with the Boxster. Equipped with Porsche's PDK double-clutch gearbox or *Doppelkupplungsgetriebe* (in German, you just keep adding letters until you get the word you want), models with the new 2.9-liter (177-cubic-inch) boxer engine require just 8.9 liters per 100 kilometers, according to the European Union standard—equal to 26.3 mpg in the United States, or 11 percent less than the previous Boxster model with Tiptronic S. And reducing fuel consumption by an even more impressive 16 percent, to 9.2 liters per 100 kilometers, or 25.5 mpg U.S., the increase in fuel economy on the 3.4-liter (207-cubic-inch) Boxster S version with PDK is even greater in comparison with its predecessor.

The Chevrolet Corvette has been America's sports car through three generations and more than half a century. Despite a slow start in 1953 and 1954, by the end of 1955, the Corvette had earned its place in the hearts, minds, and garages of American automotive enthusiasts.

The 21st century Corvette is by far the best-looking, best-handling, and fastest Detroit-bred two-seater since the legendary 427-cubic-inch, 430 horsepower 1969 L88. Today's Corvette is a high-tech work of machine art that can go from 0 to 60 in 4.2 seconds and reach a top speed that drivers in 1969 couldn't have dreamed of. Both

2010 CORVETTE GRAND SPORT

Price: $53,580

Engine: V-8

Displacement: 376 cubic inches (6.2-liters)

Output: 430 horsepower

Gearbox: Six-speed manual

Production: Still in production

the base and GS (Grand Sport) feature a standard 6.2-liter (376-cubic-inch) V-8 that cranks out 430 horsepower, a very familiar number from the good old days. Equipped with the optional dual

mode exhaust, the V-8 delivers 436 horsepower, one horse better than the 1969 L71 Corvette! The Z06 option takes the output into Ferrari territory with a 7.0-liter V-8 that produces 505 horsepower, while the extremely limited production ZR1 delivers a heart-pounding 638 horsepower from a supercharged 6.2-liter (427-cubic-inch) V-8.

Suspension and brakes are the best in Corvette history with traction control, ABS, and a standard six-speed manual with launch control. The Z06 will clip off 0 to 60 in 3.9 seconds and hit a top speed approaching 190 miles per hour (306 km/hr).

The Corvette convertible in any model configuration is the best Corvette ever, a statement that not only hints at GM's dedication to keeping one of the greatest American dreams alive, but to building a world class sports car that can hold its own against exotic imports. Consider this: the base Corvette convertible can clock 0 to 60 in 4.2 seconds, cover the quarter-mile in 12.5 seconds at 115 miles per hour (185 km/hr), and leave anything not wearing a window sticker three times its price in the dust. That's history worth making. *Photos courtesy GM Media Archive*

Did You Know?
The Corvette convertible was discontinued in 1976 and not reintroduced until 1986.

It is only fitting to end this book with the car that did so much to bring the classic postwar roadster into the modern age. Cute, quick, nimble, and fun to drive, the Mazda Miata was created as a throwback to the legendary British Triumphs, MGs, Austin-Healeys, and Jaguars—but with a very big difference: while those old machines were notoriously unreliable and lacking in many of the basic "comforts" one would expect from a car—such as side windows and watertight tops—the Miata has been a rock-solid performer since its celebrated debut in 1989. In September of that year, *Car and Driver* magazine heaped voluminous praise

2011 MAZDA MX-5 MIATA

Price: $25,450 (Touring trim option)

Engine: DOHC 16-valve four-cylinder with variable valve timing

Displacement: 2 liters (122 cubic inches)

Output: 167 horsepower (with manual transmission)

Gearbox: 6-speed close-ratio with short-throw shifter

Production: Still in production

on the new roadster: "If [a reader of this magazine] could have described his dream car—the absolute best thing he could imagine—it would have been

all too like the Mazda MX-5 Miata. But it wouldn't have been as perfect as the Mazda; no one would have dared dream of a two-seater so deft in its execution, so lacking in sports car nuisances."

Now in its third generation, the MX-5 (it's official name, although American enthusiasts continue to call it Miata) is still hailed for its near-perfect mix of simplicity and performance and is the world's most popular amateur club racing car by a wide margin. The Miata was to a young generation in the 1980s and 1990s what MGs and Triumph TRs were to Baby Boomers in the 1960s and 1970s: an affordable two-seater that could be driven every day, raced on the weekend, all the while fulfilling the dreams of young men and women who wanted to feel the rush of air flowing over the windshield but not the pinch in their pocketbook of more costly sports cars. Like the old MGB and Triumph TR6, the Miata left enough money in a driver's wallet to buy gas for a weekend road trip. For more than 20 years, Mazda has managed to keep that quintessential convertible charm safe and sound and remains one of the lowest priced, pure sports cars in the world. And that's what a convertible is supposed to be! *Photos ©Guy Spangenberg/MNAO*

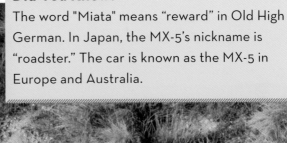

Did You Know?
The word "Miata" means "reward" in Old High German. In Japan, the MX-5's nickname is "roadster." The car is known as the MX-5 in Europe and Australia.

2011 MAZDA MX-5 MIATA

INDEX